COMBAT HAPKIDO

THE MARTIAL ART FOR THE MODERN WARRIOR

JOHN PELLEGRINI

BLACK BELT
B·O·O·K·S

COMBAT HAPKIDO

JOHN PELLEGRINI

THE MARTIAL ART FOR THE MODERN WARRIOR

Edited by Sarah Dzida, Raymond Horwitz,
Jeannine Santiago and Jon Sattler

Graphic Design by John Bodine

Photography by Rick Hustead

Demonstration Partner: David Rivas

First Printing 2009

BLACK BELT BOOKS
A Division of **OHARA** PUBLICATIONS, INC.
World Leader in Martial Arts Publications

DEDICATION

*"The fearful die a thousand deaths,
the brave only one."*

—Anonymous

This book is dedicated to all true warriors past, present and future.

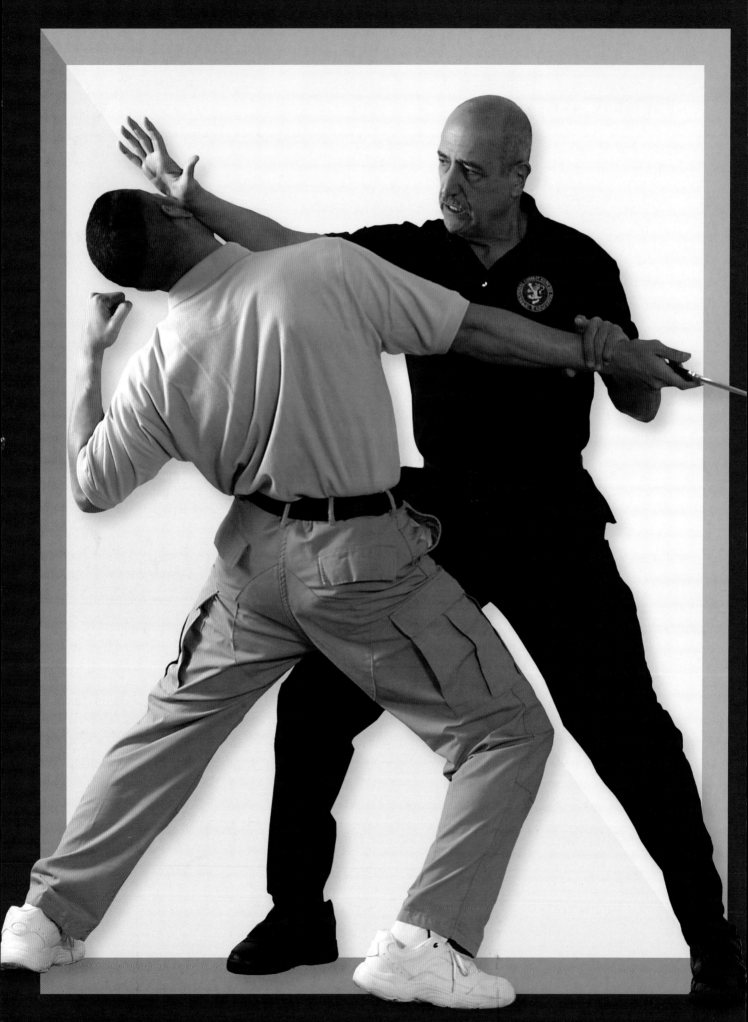

ACKNOWLEDGMENTS

The martial arts have changed my life in many positive ways, including giving me the ability for the past 25 years to turn my passion into a successful profession. They have given me the opportunity to travel the world and teach seminars in 20 countries at my last count. They have given me the opportunity to meet, befriend, train with and even teach alongside some of the greatest martial arts legends, celebrities, champions and experts in modern history. And now, they have given me the opportunity to write this book.

Therefore, with eternal gratitude in my heart, I want to thank some very special individuals who have significantly contributed to my personal growth and martial arts success:

- My parents for teaching me the importance of honesty and hard work. They have passed on, but I am sure that they would be proud to hold this book in their hands.

- My first *hapkido* teacher, the late grandmaster Michael Wollmershauser.

- My wife, Trina, for all her behind-the-scenes hard work over the years and for patiently typing this manuscript.

- My hapkido teacher, grandmaster In Sun Seo, for sharing his incredible knowledge and for his strong support and his friendship.

- *Black Belt* Executive Editor Robert W. Young, for believing in my work, and his whole staff, a friendly, generous and competent team.

- Finally, the thousands of combat hapkido students and instructors around the world for their loyalty and dedication and for making our system an important and permanent part of martial arts history.

To be sure, there have been many more individuals who have influenced me, inspired me, taught me and given me their friendship over the years, but there are too many to mention here. For that, I apologize, but their contribution is appreciated and never forgotten.

—John Pellegrini
2009

TABLE OF CONTENTS

DEDICATION 5

ACKNOWLEDGMENTS 7

INTRODUCTION 10

CHAPTER 1
THE CASE FOR SELF-DEFENSE TRAINING 13

CHAPTER 2
A BRIEF HISTORY OF HAPKIDO 19

CHAPTER 3
EVOLUTION INTO COMBAT HAPKIDO 23

CHAPTER 4
FUNDAMENTAL PRINCIPLES AND CONCEPTS 28

CHAPTER 5
STRIKING AND KICKING 37

CHAPTER 6
CLOSING THE GAP WITH TRAPPING 54

CHAPTER 7
DEFENSE AGAINST GRABS AND CHOKES 64

CHAPTER 8
DEFENSE AGAINST PUNCHES AND KICKS 107

CHAPTER 9
DEFENSE AGAINST WEAPONS 121

EPILOGUE 157

ABOUT THE AUTHOR 158

TESTIMONIALS 159

INTRODUCTION

The vast majority of people who buy a martial arts book are martial artists, but they do not all buy a book for the same reason. Depending on their level of expertise and their motivation, students of the martial arts will buy a book for the following three reasons:

- They already study that particular style and enjoy reading a book detailing its history, explaining its principles and illustrating its techniques. Although the learning of a style is best done with physical classes under a qualified instructor and, as a second choice, through DVDs, books such as this one can be a valuable and easily accessible reference tool.

- They are open-minded students who may study a particular art but are curious about or interested in another style and want to investigate it. They might also be dissatisfied with or burned out by their particular art and may be looking for something else to guide them or to enhance what they already know.

- There are also those who buy every martial arts book they can get their hands on regardless of the art or style just because they love reading anything that has to do with the martial arts and enjoy collecting them for their library.

This book will satisfy all those needs. It also must address that minority of individuals who, although not involved in the martial arts, may decide to read it. Perhaps they have decided to learn about self-defense, and their first step is to learn more about it by reading some books before choosing a particular style. Perhaps they believe that a good book and a willing partner to train with are all they need to learn how to protect themselves—although I definitely do not recommend that! Perhaps they are intrigued by the title and want to read it for the same reason many non-martial artists enjoy watching a martial arts movie.

Regardless of the reason, I believe in welcoming anything that attracts and sparks interest in the topic of self-defense. All fighting systems, martial arts and warrior disciplines, whether ancient or modern, have a story that deserves to be told. Their history, lineage and technical qualities are important, and so are the achievements of their founders. Their written records, even in this age of the Internet, are an indispensable part of the fabric of combat culture, and they are the most permanent legacy of those who have dedicated their lives to teaching warriors how to survive.

However, readers must be honest and realistic in their approach and expectations by understanding that a book is just a conduit of information and has its limitations. The martial arts are not mere academic endeavors such as history or literature that can be learned with books only. This book should be approached as a framework, a blueprint of combat *hapkido*. But we must remember that the blueprint is not the building. Combat hapkido and all other self-defense systems can only be mastered by physical practice under the expert guidance of a qualified instructor.

With that said, over the last 20 years, combat hapkido has gained popularity and a huge following, becoming one of the fastest-growing self-defense systems in the world. Hundreds of instructors are teaching combat hapkido in large and small martial arts schools, clubs and military bases in more than a dozen countries, and more than 2,000 black belts have been certified. This book has been eagerly awaited by these students, and I am confident that they will welcome it not only as a source of pride in their chosen system but also as a practical tool to improve and deepen their understanding of combat hapkido. I also believe that all martial arts practitioners and individuals interested in self-defense will enjoy this book and benefit from it. I humbly offer it as part of my legacy and as my contribution to the warrior community.

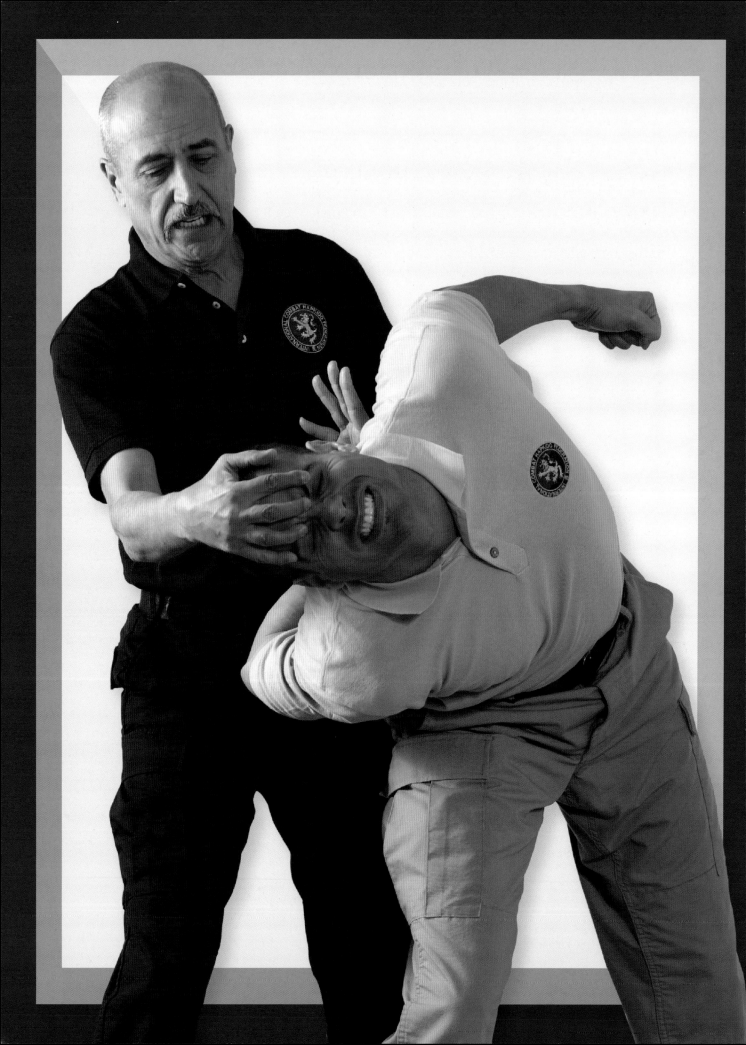

CHAPTER 1
THE CASE FOR SELF-DEFENSE TRAINING

All martial arts originated and were developed with only one objective: physical combat. For many centuries, different cultures have recognized the need to study and structure fighting methods, although initially, these methods were only intended for and limited to the warrior class. Modern practitioners of the arts often overlook or are unaware of the true meaning of the word "martial." Derived from Mars, the Roman god of war, martial simply means "of war" or "warrior." So the martial arts are the arts of the warrior. Although in most cultures, Asian as well as Western, games and contests were created to test the skills of the warriors, to prove the effectiveness of the techniques or to entertain the crowds, the martial arts were not developed for sport and were never meant to be primarily as such.

Becoming a strong athlete was a desirable and expected byproduct (maybe even a requirement) of martial training, but it was not its ultimate purpose. The rigorous and sometimes brutal training, as well as the methodology and rituals associated with practice and the occasional trials, were all designed to forge the fighter into a superior, skillful, courageous and reliable warrior. To see how far people have moved away from that original intent today, you only have to look at the storefront window of the average shopping-mall martial arts school. The signs promise great benefits: fitness, self-confidence, self-discipline, respect, even fun and better academic grades. Most also casually mention self-defense, but it appears to be almost an afterthought or an incidental perk. This change of attitude and perspective was probably inevitable and commercially necessary. Modern culture, laws and social structure require the transformation of the martial arts into a benign, user-friendly, nonmilitaristic activity that is available and beneficial to men, women and children of all walks of life. What was once reserved for the warrior class is now a family activity open to everyone, and there is nothing inherently wrong with that.

I do not lament or disapprove of this transformation. I just want to make clear the fact that true self-defense training has taken a back seat, or is even totally neglected, by the majority of today's martial arts schools. It can be argued that in today's civilized, high-tech society, personal fighting and survival skills are not as important or necessary as they once were. Military forces have changed, too, and the likelihood of individual, unarmed hand-to-hand combat is considered remote, which therefore reduces or even eliminates the need for martial arts training.

I disagree strongly with those premises. In the case of civilians, understand that in the United States, for example, there are 600,000 police officers for a population of 320 million. (The U.S. government releases statistics like this every year, and they tend to fluctuate.) Their function is primarily reactive, meaning that they will arrive on the scene *after* a crime has been committed and a person has already been victimized. Just reflect for a moment on the fact that in the United States, there is a violent crime committed every 22 seconds and a property crime every three seconds. And the situation is not much better in most of the rest of the world (and in many places, it is much worse). So it would behoove everyone to learn how to protect themselves, their families and their hard-earned property, and now that martial arts training is no longer restricted to the warrior class and is finally easily accessible to everyone, it would seem logical and practical that many people would want to learn self-defense.

The law-enforcement community, with its very specific needs, requirements and unique mission, would also greatly benefit from consistent and competent training in defensive tactics. Among the many benefits that police forces would gain from increased defensive training would be less reliance on deadly weapons, fewer charges of police brutality and the excessive use of force, fewer injuries and deaths of officers, a decrease in civil litigations, and a more positive public image. Finally, in the case of military personnel, although the weapons, tactics and methods of modern warfare have changed dramatically, there is still a need for effective combatives training. Having personally trained troops from different branches of the armed forces at many bases around the world, including Colombia, Afghanistan and Iraq, I can attest that the training is useful, relevant and always welcome. Paradoxically, some of the changes that occur in the modern conduct of warfare demand an increase in professional combatives training rather than a decrease. Strict and complex rules of engagement, everyday interaction with the civilian population, increase of police-like functions, the handling of prisoners, and the presence of media and neutral observers in combat zones require the modern soldier to possess empty-hand skills once thought obsolete for a war environment.

In conclusion, self-defense training, in all its customizations for specific groups, is still relevant, important and, in many cases, necessary. That brings us to the current trend of reality-based styles. Is it a return of the arts to their original "martial" meaning and a revival of scientific self-defense training? Or is it just a fad to be exploited at the expense of a gullible public?

The "Reality-Based" Trend

In the past few years, there has been a proliferation of ads in martial arts magazines that promote a variety of "reality-based" styles and systems. While the terminology is new and trendy, the substance is as old as the history of the martial arts. As I have previously stated, the only reason fighting disciplines were developed was to train warriors for real combat. It is almost amusing to observe that there is a label to distinguish reality-based styles from … what? Fantasy-based styles? Unfortunately, that distinction is all too often correct. Most of today's traditional martial arts have long abandoned any pretense of teaching realistic, street-effective techniques, and all sport-based styles are just that: sports. So even though, at first glance, reality-based self-defense appears to be a redundant phrase, it is actually accurate. That label, if honestly applied, defines the material that will be taught, its methodology and its true objective, therefore giving consumers a choice in making a decision on what to study. Not everyone considers self-defense a priority, and many people around the world practice martial arts for a great variety of reasons—from stress relief to spiritual enlightenment and from fitness to championship glory. By clearly identifying systems as reality-based, instructors will attract only those individuals who truly want or need serious self-defense training.

One word of caution, however: Picking up a trendy and commercially rewarding label and sticking it on something is easy. Just because it claims to be reality-based does not necessarily make it so. By capitalizing on the success of veteran instructors who have paid their dues by working hard to develop sound, combat-tested systems, a bunch of wannabes have recently jumped on the bandwagon, making phony claims and attempting to cash in on the popularity of reality-based training. I believe in free enterprise, and I welcome talented and honest instructors who can make contributions to the advancement of the science of combat. What I deplore is the sudden appearance of self-declared experts who make unverifiable claims (such as having trained elite units of the Israeli army, Russian *spetsnaz*, SWAT teams and Navy SEALs) and shamelessly promote repackaged techniques as the ultimate, secret, unbeatable, instantly deadly, never-before-seen fighting system. I am almost tempted to say that people who fall for such outlandish, absurd hype deserve to waste their time and money, but the truth is that those unscrupulous clowns hurt our industry and put their students in danger. Acquiring effective, tested fighting skills and building the warrior mind-set requires time and effort under the guidance of an experienced instructor and cannot be purchased by sending a few dollars to a P.O. Box. As always, if it seems too good to be true, it probably is.

Combat *hapkido* is a true martial art in the sense that it has always been about reality-based self-defense, even years before the term became part of society's lexicon. It was always intended for students who are sincere and serious about developing the warrior mind-set and willing to make the necessary investment and sacrifices, instead of looking for a nonexistent quick fix and instant gratification. In a world where violent crimes and terrorism are a grim presence in our daily lives, reality-based self-defense training can be a powerful tool for personal safety and a more secure society. But you must choose wisely.

Modern Gladiators

No discussion about self-defense would be complete without the inclusion of another controversial topic: the sport aspect of the martial arts. The rising popularity of spectator events collectively known as "no holds barred" has had a definite and irreversible impact on the martial arts industry in terms of physical training and public perception. As I have previously mentioned, contests have always been part of warrior training. The Olympic Games of ancient Greece included martial activities such as wrestling, boxing and javelin throwing. Rome, of course, was infamous for its brutal gladiator matches to the death. Jousting, fencing, archery and equestrian contests also have their roots in warrior training. For thousands of years, every culture on every continent has created some form of fighting sport. So what you watch today on television is not a new phenomenon. People have always been eager to observe physical combat, armed or unarmed, with rules or without them.

The modern sport aspect of the martial arts began with judo, which was introduced as a safer variation of *jujutsu*. Its founder, Jigoro Kano, wanted a less dangerous way to practice and enjoy the art and, by reducing the chance of injuries, make it accessible to more people, including children. Judo was the first Asian martial art to be accepted as an Olympic sport. The 1970s saw the rise of different aspects of karate competition, and many of today's martial arts icons and legends, such as Chuck Norris, Joe Lewis, Bill Wallace, Jeff Smith and Don Wilson, achieved their fame because of their exciting performances in those championships.

Beginning in the 1980s, the Korean art of *taekwondo* started its unprecedented climb in popularity, and today, it is the most widely practiced Asian art in the world. Its tremendous popularity must be partly attributed to its easy adaptability into a sport. In fact, today in Korea, taekwondo is classified as a "martial sport." There are hundreds of taekwondo tournaments and championships held every weekend in the United States and around the world. And taekwondo has also become an Olympic sport.

The 1980s also saw the beginning of a phenomenon that can be called "the Gracie Revolution." This very talented family introduced Brazilian *jiu-jitsu* to the world, and the martial arts would never be the same. Their system became extremely popular and commercially successful because of its exposure in the Ultimate Fighting Championship and the Gracie family's legendary winning record.

Although popularized and promoted today as a sport, Gracie jiu-jitsu was forged in the streets of Brazil by tough fighters who confronted each other with few or no rules. It has proved itself as a superb fighting discipline for those with the physical abilities necessary for its rigorous training. On the technical level, what Brazilian jiu-jitsu (the Gracies, the Machados and other styles), *vale tudo*, combat *sambo* and other grappling styles revealed was the inadequacy or total lack of ground-fighting skills in most traditional martial arts. For exposing this glaring weakness to the world, the Gracie family deserves the credit.

I personally do not believe the advertising hype (now held by many as fact) that 95 percent of street fights wind up on the ground. There are simply no reliable surveys or professionally researched statistics to buttress that claim. Many fights wind up on the ground, of course, and because of that, no seriously effective reality-based self-defense system can afford to neglect the inclusion of ground-fighting skills in its curriculum.

Unfortunately, Graciemania and the UFC have also had a negative impact on many instructors who have become obsessed with ground fighting at the expense of all other training. This near fixation has caused many to practice, teach and embrace ground grappling exclusively with very little to no thought given to stand-up skills. To them, the sport aspect of Brazilian jiu-jitsu had proved almost unbeatable in the ring, and it followed that it was truly the ultimate fighting method. Consequently, these instructors believe there is no valid reason to waste time learning anything else. I consider this an unwise and unproductive approach to teaching reality-based self-defense. Without official documentation, we will probably never know whether 95 percent, 65 percent or 35 percent of fights wind up on the ground, but I agree that a person should be prepared, first by training on how to *avoid* going to the ground and then on how to survive while on the ground.

This brief review of the sport aspect of the martial arts is important because there is a misconception that equates athletic prowess and winning in competition with self-defense skills. Of course, those two attributes are not mutually exclusive and can coexist in the same individual, but one does not guarantee the other. To put it bluntly, there are many tournament champions who could not last 10 seconds in a street fight. Conversely, there are seasoned street fighters who, given the rules, could not go one round in a ring. Fair enough. But the problem is that self-defense is always about fighting bad guys in the street with no rules. It is not about scoring points on respectful, mentally balanced, disciplined competitors of your chosen art.

Some readers at this point may argue that the athletes who compete in events such as the UFC are awesome fighters and would have no problem defeating an attacker in a street confrontation. I agree, and personally, I would not go in the ring with any of them—I am too old for that anyway. I also would not want to confront them outside the ring. And that is not just because of their technical expertise but mostly because of their level of physical conditioning. Let's face it: None of these fighters are in their 60s (like me). They are strong, fit and able (and willing) to tolerate a tremendous amount of physical punishment. The reason the average person, including the average martial arts student, would not stand a chance with one of those fighters is simply training. Those competitors train hard for several hours a day, every day, with only one goal in mind: to win in the ring. Their training focuses exclusively on that goal and is designed accordingly.

This single-minded approach results in specialization. They become tough, hard, fearless fighters who are willing to do what it takes to be the best in the ring. This modality is, of course, not for the majority of the population. While millions like to watch these modern gladiator events, very few people are willing, able or interested in taking up that kind of training to pursue a competitor's life. Established fighters of the UFC and similar events could and would, easily and successfully, apply their great skills and superb conditioning in any reality-based self-defense situation. However, the same cannot be said about most competitors of other martial arts. Those weekend warriors who compete in tournaments by performing beautiful *kata* or sparring with safety gear in a highly controlled environment cannot, for the most part, translate their techniques into reality-based self-defense skills. The nasty, brutal, explosive nature of a street attack is physically and psychologically so removed from that kind of competition (and the type of training associated with it) as to be of little or no value in self-defense.

You can ask the question, Is a taekwondo or karate competitor better off in a street attack than someone with no martial arts training at all? The answer is yes, but not for the reason you may think. Anyone with some martial arts training has an advantage in a self-defense situation over someone who has never practiced martial arts, but not because of his participation in the sport aspect of the arts. The advantage lies in the martial artist's superior understanding of the human body, proper striking techniques, manipulation of joints, knowledge of pressure points and general defensive strategies. The untrained individual not only lacks those attributes but also does not possess that special warrior mind-set developed in training. Therefore, if you need to defend yourself, having some martial arts training is probably preferable than no training at all.

Finally, to have a clear and complete picture of the differences between sport competition and reality-based self-defense, I must mention—and this applies to all martial contests, including the "no holds barred"—that even the most ferocious legal competitions have rules. There are weight classes, time limits, referees, confined environments and rules that don't allow access to weapons and many techniques, such as eye gouging, groin strikes, head-butting and biting. Ironically, those are some of the techniques freely and frequently used by the bad guys in the street—and also the very same useful techniques for the good guys to defend themselves. Additionally, street attacks will often involve multiple assailants, sometimes of much larger size, and the use of weapons: guns, knives, lead pipes, broken bottles, etc.

Previously, you examined the differences between traditional martial arts and reality-based self-defense systems such as combat hapkido. Martial sport is the third side of this triangle. Although at times overlapping, mingling or complementing each other, these three sides of physical combat (traditional, reality-based, sport) are unique. They each provide different experiences, offer different benefits and achieve different objectives for different purposes. Although a student can train in and play with all three sides—many have, and it has its benefits—I am a firm believer in specialization. Only by seriously and completely focusing your training in one area can you become truly proficient. Unfortunately, no training in the world can ever guarantee survival in a deadly situation, but reality-based self-defense training, as opposed to most traditional arts and martial sports, provides the best technical preparation and all-important warrior mind-set necessary to fight back.

CHAPTER 2
A BRIEF HISTORY OF HAPKIDO

Over the past 2,000 years, the Korean people have developed several fighting systems and martial disciplines, which have evolved into modern taekwondo, *tang soo do*, hapkido, *kook sool*, *hwa rang do*, etc. Hundreds of years of trade, war, military occupation and cultural exchange between Korea and its neighbors of China and Japan have resulted in cross-pollination, or a mutual influence and blending of styles and techniques. It is now virtually impossible to state with certainty which techniques are truly Korean, Chinese or Japanese in origin. In addition, the lack of records and the abundance of conflicting testimonies all but ensure sketchy and biased accounts of traditional martial arts.

The most widely accepted version of the origins of hapkido is that it was founded by Choi Yong-sul. There is really no reliable information on Choi's life, but it is generally reported that he developed the system by combining native Korean fighting methods with Japanese *daito-ryu aikijujutsu*.

I can only speculate on what Choi's purpose was in creating hapkido. It is known that he spent about 30 years studying aikijujutsu in Japan, and it is safe to assume that during that time, he developed a strong love for the martial arts. After returning to Korea, in 1945, he was certainly eager to share his knowledge and his passion for martial training with his native people. He found his opportunity in a fortuitous encounter with his wealthy employer, Suh Bok-sup, who studied judo. When Suh learned about Choi's background and witnessed his skills during a fight at the distillery he owned, he financed a *dojang*, or training hall, and hired Choi to be the instructor. Suh became Choi's first student.

Had it not been for the extremely brutal 35-year Japanese occupation of Korea and the consequent hatred of all things Japanese on the part of the Korean people, Choi would have probably been perfectly content to teach aikijujutsu or the generic name *yawara* (self-defense); hapkido would not have come into existence. Political and ethnic necessities demanded that Choi "Koreanize" the system and introduce it with a new name. Details on this process of Koreanization, both in name and in technical attributes, are extremely sketchy. What is known and ultimately relevant is that around 1948, Choi and a few of his original students started using the word "hapkido" and started teaching this new hybrid martial art. For example, he modified *aikido* sword-defense techniques to better fit the grabbing attacks his students would meet on the street. He also added Korean-style hand and foot strikes to bolster hapkido's effectiveness. Another undeniable fact is that post-World War II Korea was a dangerous place with a collapsed social infrastructure, rampant crime and pervasive poverty. Therefore, Choi was teaching an extremely effective, never-before-seen system of self-defense at the right time and place. Hapkido was born because history placed Choi at the convergence of unique political and social events.

The literal translation of the word "hapkido" is tied closely to that of the Japanese word "aikido."

HAP—To combine, to unite, to coordinate, to join—AI
KI—Internal power, dynamic energy, life force—KI
DO—The way, the system, the method—DO

Each syllable has several corresponding English words because Eastern languages express thoughts, ideas and concepts differently than Western ones. This results in translations that only approximate the original meaning. The Korean characters for hapkido directly translate in Japanese as aikido 合気道 and vice versa.

Although both arts share common origins in aikijujutsu, don't confuse the two arts or consider them the same because they are not. Aikido was founded in Japan in 1941, and founder Morihei Uyeshiba had a different philosophy than Choi's and implemented different techniques. Specifically, Uyeshiba de-emphasized and drastically reduced kicking and striking techniques in favor of a gentler, flowing redirection of an attack because of his religious background and spiritually pacifist attitude. To be sure, the throws and joint locks of aikido are as painful and devastating as hapkido's—after all, both arts come from the same aikijujutsu roots—but the whole approach of aikido is one of nonviolence, with wider circular movements and little close-quarters engagement.

Taking all this into consideration, hapkido's foundation rests on three universal principles:

- **The water principle** directs practitioners to penetrate the defense of an opponent by flowing in, over, around and under his attacks.

- **The circular-motion principle** directs practitioners to gain and impart momentum by moving in a circular manner. This helps control the balance and kinetic energy of the attacker.

- **The harmony principle** directs practitioners to remain relaxed, flexible and not tense. They learn to not meet force with force.

While these principles are essential to the art, they are not unique to hapkido. Even the most superficial research reveals that they are embedded in the practice of aikido and its progenitor, aikijujutsu. Other "soft" styles, particularly of Chinese origin, also incorporate variations of these principles to some extent.

Today, there are many styles of hapkido and associations that govern it. Some styles have produced forms that are required knowledge for advancement. Other styles emphasize high kicking, including jumping and flying kicks. Others are still more heavily influenced by judo or aikido and emphasize throwing skills.

Over the last 35 years, hapkido has become more well-known and has joined the mainstream martial arts community. In the United States, since the art's first mass exposure in the

1971 movie *Billy Jack* (choreographed by the late Bong Soo Han), hapkido is generally offered as a secondary art to the more popular taekwondo or tang soo do. However, hapkido's future continues to be promising, and most likely, its popularity will only continue to increase.

More than 40 years after, combat hapkido was introduced to the United States, and its purpose was the same as the original art: to teach effective, realistic self-defense. The difference, however, is that combat hapkido was born in a very different crucible. The social, legal, cultural and technological environment of the United States in the early 1990s was very different from Korea in the 1940s. Hence the need for an evolution as well as the development of a specific new identity that reflected modern times in a drastically different culture.

Black Belt (March 1972)

Suh Bok-sup

I had the privilege of interviewing Suh Bok-sup in April 2000 as part of my own personal research in the history of *hapkido*. This gentle and extremely unassuming man was eager to share anecdotes and answer my questions about the development of hapkido. He was clear on the fact that Choi initially taught a syllabus of only 100 techniques; that Choi

Photo courtesy of John Pellegrini

Yong-sul did not teach *kata*; that there were no jumping, spinning high kicks; and that Choi did not initially intend to found a new martial art. He simply wanted to teach self-defense, using the knowledge he had acquired in Japan. The Koreanization of the art with the coining of the name "hapkido" and certain technical modifications happened gradually and were the result of ethnic and political necessities.

While I have the utmost respect and admiration for professor Suh Bok-sup and I consider him an important historical figure of the martial arts, ultimately, I cannot verify with certainty the accuracy of every detail. Aside from the possible distortion in translation, our conversation was about events that had occurred about 45 years earlier. Memories tend to fade, and I must also allow for the possibility of a little personal bias to subtly influence the story. However, the main facts are undisputable, and most important, they are firsthand accounts from an unimpeachable source who also was not only there when hapkido was born but was instrumental in its creation.

CHAPTER 3
EVOLUTION INTO COMBAT HAPKIDO

Recent martial arts history offers a variety of famous examples of talented practitioners forgoing tradition to follow their own instincts, aspirations and convictions. The first that comes to mind is, of course, Bruce Lee, who after studying traditional *wing chun*, went on to create his own style, known as *jeet kune do*. Lee became a leading advocate of the eclectic approach, rejecting what he called the "classical mess" of traditional martial arts. Although he was criticized by some, Lee became a legend and arguably one of the most admired and respected martial artists of all time. And he was not the only one to dare break with tradition. Ed Parker modernized the art of *kenpo* and introduced his system of American kenpo, Wally Jay created his small-circle *jujitsu*, and Remy Presas blended several Philippine styles into modern *arnis*. Many more examples could be provided, but the point is that this eclectic approach is not a rare anomaly; it has always been an important component of the engine of martial arts development across the cultural spectrum.

Martial arts history also provides an intriguing paradox to the conflict between the traditional and eclectic group. Students of a particular style, unlike those mentioned above, tend to invoke tradition, vowing to strictly follow the teachings of the style's founder. But one must ask, What about the founder of that system? Was he or she not an innovator? A pioneer? Maybe even a rebel who, after studying someone else's martial art, broke with tradition and decided to change it, modify it or even, dare I say, improve it? All founders are, by definition, eclectic creators who structure and codify a body of knowledge acquired by them from someone else and select, arrange and organize that knowledge into a system reflecting their personal beliefs, experiences, priorities and environment. So the paradox is that all traditional arts started as eclectic systems and that, after time, some of their practitioners decided or will decide to begin an evolutionary process of the now-traditional arts. They will create in turn new styles, which students will in time again come to view and accept as traditional arts.

The development of combat hapkido has followed a path similar to many other eclectic systems. It started with the journey of an individual—me—through the traditional martial arts, which in this case were karate, taekwondo, hapkido and aikido. While I found my time with these styles as a student and teacher very rewarding, even life-changing, I began to realize that many techniques were quite impractical for modern self-defense applications. I also noticed that many of my mature students were struggling with the most acrobatic movements, such as high kicks and traditional throws and breakfalls.

I did not wake up one morning experiencing an epiphany that prompted me to abandon traditional study in favor of reality-based training. Instead, the transition between traditional and eclectic camps was a gradual process dictated by the unique requirements and experiences of my work in law enforcement.

From this work, I saw that a different skill set was called for than that which I had acquired in my traditional training. Unlike the one-on-one training of a traditional dojang, law enforcement must control and apprehend individuals who are resisting arrest (mostly unarmed but sometimes with weapons) without using excessive force that may result in injuries and while protecting themselves and others. A very complex and delicate balance existed between the safe and successful performance of my duty as a law-enforcement officer and the moral and legal constraints I had to operate within. I discovered that many strikes and kicks of traditional arts were not acceptable in that context. I also found that most traditional blocks were too slow and ineffective and that many other techniques were too complicated for instinctive employment—the defender had to instinctively execute the technique under highly unpredictable circumstances. My independent research led me on a path of discovery for a more practical, effective and realistic method.

This ensuing analysis convinced me that changes were needed, and I set out to structure a new curriculum. To differentiate this style, I coined the name "combat hapkido." I guess it would have been just as easy to invent a totally new name, thus avoiding a lot of controversy. But that was not my desire, nor was it my objective. I wanted to continue promoting and teaching hapkido. I wanted to honor and respect the art that had changed my life. I wanted everyone to know where the system came from, acknowledge its roots and give credit where it belonged. So I simply did what many others before me had done: I founded a new style that would represent my expression of the art, my contribution to its evolution and what I believed to be necessary changes to its technical attributes.

In the context of my system, "combat" simply refers to realistic self-defense as opposed to a sport or traditional art. But calling an art by a new name and claiming that it is a different style is obviously not enough. Superficial changes do not contribute to the evolution of an art. The true evolution of an art lies unequivocally in its conceptual attributes, scientific principles and technical applications—exactly what one will find in the study of combat hapkido.

So with this in mind, I eliminated what I considered to be many outdated techniques and flashy movements. For example, traditional hapkido and many other traditional styles paid a lot of attention to postures, stances and movements, but combat hapkido recognized that these postures, stances and movements were relevant to another time and place. I also eliminated the recognizable high, jumping and spinning kicks of the art because they were too flashy or acrobatic for safe application in any of the martial arts contexts discussed in Chapter 1: civilian self-defense, law-enforcement defensive tactics and military combatives.

But I also added new material, including basic trapping techniques as commonly found in jeet kune do, in order to close the gap at close quarters. Trapping techniques not only brought an exceptional technical attribute to combat hapkido that was not present in the original art but also gave the system a truly unique identity. No one had attempted to blend elements of jeet kune do with hapkido. Of course, the controversy of blending jeet kune do with hapkido has been great, but I considered and still consider it as one of the most useful and interesting contributions to the development and expression of this system.

(Ironically, in March 1999, my hapkido teacher, grandmaster In Sun Seo, granted combat hapkido official *kwan* or style status in the World Kido Federation, an organization chartered by the Korean government to preserve, promote and keep records of all legitimate styles of Korean martial arts. This accreditation, which is usually awarded only to traditional arts, firmly established combat hapkido as a historically recognized contributor to the evolution of Korean martial arts. Combat hapkido's official Korean name is *chon-tu kwan hapkido*.)

In developing combat hapkido, I also addressed other issues, such as the lack of ground-fighting techniques. I embarked on extensive research into ground-fighting systems, training with and seeking guidance and expertise from some of the best instructors in the world. I placed one of my most talented senior black belts, David Rivas, in charge of the project, and within a few years, we were able to develop a complete technical course of ground fighting that emphasized self-defense and not a competitive grappling sport, like that found in the Ultimate Fighting Championship. We called it Combat Hapkido Ground Survival.

And of course, besides the above-mentioned modifications, I retained the core of hapkido by keeping the main body of techniques such as joint locks, pressure points, strikes, kicks, etc. Once again, I did not invent a new art. I just modernized and modified it according to my experience of it.

I also saw no reason to eliminate or diminish the timeless and scientifically sound principles discussed in Chapter 2. They remain a solid bedrock for all the techniques currently taught in combat hapkido. To examine them with a simple, modern approach, I'll illustrate them as follows:

- **The Water Principle.** Imagine a flowing stream and then imagine placing a boulder in the middle of that stream. You will observe that the water will keep flowing, finding its way over, under and around the boulder. The water principle teaches you to not be the boulder but to be the water—flowing and unstoppable—toward the attacker by passing and overcoming his attack and his defense. On a psychological level, this principle also teaches practitioners to confront life problems and challenges by finding creative solutions and strategies so that they are allowed to move forward.

- **The Circular Principle.** The human body is designed to resist linear energy but cannot easily counter circular energy. It is simple physics. By redirecting the linear energy of an attacker in a circular manner, you not only cause the energy to dissipate, but you also disrupt the balance (equilibrium) of the attacker, allowing you to manipulate his body to your advantage.

- **The Harmony Principle.** Also known as the nonresistance principle, this often-misunderstood concept does not imply passivity or the lack of active resistance to an attack. It simply states that you will be more efficient and conserve your energy by not opposing force with (linear) force. An often-used example of this principle is the directive: "When pushed, pull; when pulled, push." Harmony in this case means blending your energy with and not against your attacker's energy for maximum results with minimum effort.

I cannot stress enough that these principles are not stand-alone pieces of theoretical knowledge. They are inextricably connected as part of a dynamic, integrated continuum.

Finally, I evaluated each technique in order to ensure that, without losing effectiveness in the real world, they would be as "legally friendly" as possible. It did not make sense to me that combat-hapkido students would avoid the hospital only to wind up in jail, and in today's society, that was a major concern. I spent about two years introducing and presenting this new system to the media. And through demonstrations, clinics and seminars, it received a positive response, but not without some controversy.

The time was right, and the martial arts community was intrigued with combat hapkido. In 1992, I officially founded the International Combat Hapkido Federation, a necessary governing body to formalize and regulate the system with the sole authority to issue rank certifications and instructor licenses. However, the journey is not over. Combat hapkido will always be a work in progress, constantly improving, evolving and never stagnant. The style has also generated several subsystems, which have been custom-designed for specific groups such as the military and law-enforcement communities. The goal still remains the same: to exist at the cutting edge of the martial arts evolution.

Combat Hapkido Subsystems

Not counting my early teenage forays into the martial arts as serious or relevant, my first truly formative experience in the fighting arts came during my service in the Italian army from 1968 to 1969. Because I was part of an elite airborne unit, it was my good fortune to receive advanced training in unarmed combatives. (In those days, it was called hand-to-hand combat.) I later discovered that what I was learning was a modified and simplified form of *jujutsu*. One of the things that impressed me the most was how easily and effectively a smaller person could take down a larger opponent. It did not require a great physique or exceptional muscular strength. It was ideal for me; I knew I was hooked and I couldn't get enough of it. I guess that experience was what sparked my lifelong passion for the martial arts.

Over the next 20 years, I continued training, studying and eventually teaching martial arts, primarily to the civilian market. My connection to the military was never too far from my heart and mind, but I was teaching other instructors' traditional arts. I had few opportunities to interact with the military community. For several years, the same combat *hapkido* system was successfully taught to civilians, law-enforcement and military personnel. But with more experience and research, I decided to separate the single curriculum into three different subsystems, each with its own organization, certification and curriculum. This was done to better address the specific needs, requirements and legal issues of each group. We did not, however, invent new techniques every time. We just identified, selected and classified the most appropriate and relevant to the specific missions. By customizing combat hapkido to different audiences, the system became better able to service their needs and produce better results. Like I always say, self-defense is not "one size fits all."

It was not until this process was completed that I became heavily involved with training troops at military bases in the United States and around the world, beginning with my first seminar at Ramstein Air Force Base in Germany in 1994. The reason combat hapkido became so popular with the military is because it was created with them in mind. I consciously and constantly focused on my objective that the techniques and the methodology be relevant and applicable to military personnel in or out of a theater of operations.

In the particular case of the military, I had to address issues such as the equipment carried by the troops, the terrain, the types of weapons, the rules of engagement, the kind of threat, etc.

This understanding is the key to providing sound and meaningful training to our troops. In other words, combat hapkido training is something they can and will use as opposed to traditional movements or sport techniques they will never need or employ. Combat hapkido's reputation grew in the military community, culminating in several prestigious and exciting assignments: Office of Naval Intelligence in Washington, D.C., in 2007, Afghanistan in 2006, Colombia in 2008 and Iraq in 2008. It is always an honor and a privilege to work with the military, and it has been one of most rewarding aspects of my martial arts career.

CHAPTER 4
FUNDAMENTAL PRINCIPLES AND CONCEPTS

Combat hapkido is about self-defense in the street—wearing regular shoes and clothes and without the benefit of 30 minutes of stretching exercises. The primary directive of its strikes and kicks is that they use certain principles for only one reason: speed.

As previously stated, some of the underlying principles of combat hapkido are common to many other arts and are used in the same way. The difference in the integration of those principles lies in the degree of emphasis that is placed on each of them during training. As an example, principles such as economy of movement or the balance disruption may be mentioned and even briefly illustrated in other martial arts, but they are not strongly emphasized and constantly reinforced as they are in combat hapkido. Other principles, such as the lower center of gravity or the vulnerable anatomy, are often overemphasized by other martial arts, thus making defenses less instinctive, more complicated and slower.

In combat hapkido, all the principles to be discussed in this chapter are considered vital to a successful defense. These concepts should not be viewed as stand-alone elements or isolated instances in which they are called into use for a specific need. They must instead be viewed as being integrated in every movement of every technique.

Body Mechanics

Unlike traditional arts that pay a lot of attention to posture and stances, combat hapkido has no formal stances. Students instead are taught to adopt a simple and effective defensive position that offers maximum protection to vulnerable areas. This position is not specific, and it offers basic guidelines to protect you. The following is a list of these guidelines:

- **Relax your body.** Tensing muscles burns more fuel, causing you to quickly become winded and run out of energy. It also slows down reactive movements and impedes the smooth flow of techniques. A relaxed body also makes you look less threatening to an opponent, whereas a traditional martial arts posture may actually inflame the situation and prevent a peaceful resolution.

- **Maintain a lower center of gravity.** This subtle but effective grounding is accomplished by keeping the distance between your feet at a little more than shoulder-width apart. You also want to bend your knees and widen your base. By maintaining this lower center of gravity, you make it much harder (or even impossible) for the attacker to push, pull, throw or manipulate your balance.

- **Keep your elbows close.** Don't extend your elbows away from the body because this affects the power you can employ. It also compromises the structural balance and integrity of the personal defensive perimeter, exposing your center mass and making it easier for the attacker to hit you in the ribs or other vital organs. Of course, there are movements (such as when delivering a strike) that require the elbows to temporarily extend away from the body, but these movements should be transitional in nature, using the fastest speed for recovery.

- **Hold your hands "softly."** Your hands should be in front of you in a guard stance (like a boxer) but in a relaxed, soft manner with open hands.

There are also a few principles of movement that are adhered to in combat hapkido.

- **Economy of movement** is the first. This dictum is commonly attributed to Bruce Lee, and it has become one of the core concepts in combat hapkido. It refers to how wide, long, flowery, wasteful, exaggerated movements are ultimately dangerous in real fight situations. They slow down and telegraph your techniques to an opponent who is planning to harm you. Economy of movement also narrows the choices you have in a fight. This takes away the dilemma of choosing between the right and wrong technique in a volatile situation. The one choice you have is enough, and this aspect is deeply and consistently integrated into the entire combat-hapkido system.

- **Hip rotation** is the second and the often-overlooked power delivery system for movement. The torque of the hips performs a vital function in the level of power being delivered to the target when executing kicks, strikes and joint locking. The torque of the hips also greatly assists the generation of circular energy required in most of combat hapkido's techniques. Because the hips connect the upper body to the lower body, their importance in maintaining balance, controlling mobility and generating power cannot be overstated.

- **Displacement** is the third and refers to the act of removing your body from a direct line of attack. It allows you to use the attacker's momentum against him. Displacement is possible primarily against a linear attack (such as a jab) and is accomplished with minimum movement in a slightly diagonal direction toward the attacker. This also results in the attacker's strike hitting empty space instead of a solid target, causing the attacker to lose some or all of his balance.

Combining the body mechanics and movement principles that are described and applying them consistently will give you a true and solid foundation that will facilitate and enhance every technique.

The Energetic Aspect

Most martial artists are familiar with the words *qi*, *chi* and *ki*. (All different spellings and pronunciations refer to the same concept.) This concept is of the existence of an elusive energetic force that can be developed, controlled and directed for healing and physical combat. It is virtually impossible to render a literal translation of the word "ki" in English. It has been defined as life force, internal power, universal energy, etc. It may be all those or something else entirely that people are not yet able to understand with their present knowledge. For the most part, Western science and medicine have rejected the possibility of the existence of ki, dismissing the subject as based on mystical and esoteric beliefs that cannot be verified by scientific methods. On the other hand, the absolute, factual acceptance of the reality of ki is at the foundation of Eastern medicine and many martial arts.

Combat-hapkido practitioners accept as fact that ki exists even if it cannot be definitively demonstrated and proved by Western science. In fact, "ki" is actually one of the three words that make up the name of this book's art: hap-KI-do. Combat hapkido doesn't, however, attribute any mystical or supernatural properties to this energy. Instead, ki is considered another dimension of the self that people don't fully and properly understand. Because the use of ki in self-defense is mostly concerned with the flow and transfer of energy, combat hapkido focuses on that. Students are encouraged to pursue activities like *tai chi* or yoga in order to develop their awareness and improve their control of ki.

Here are some other energetic aspects of combat hapkido:

- **Live hand** refers to how the practitioner holds his hand; instead of making a fist, he opens his hand and spreads the fingers in an energetic but not stiff or tense manner. This is important to do especially if an attacker grabs your wrist. Making a fist in that situation has the effect of bottling up ki energy and restricting its free flow. A purely anatomical byproduct of the live hand is also the fact that the two bones of the forearm—the radius and ulna—spread out slightly, making a grab more difficult to maintain; your wrist becomes larger to grab. You'll also see the live hand employed in many strikes and joint locks.

- **Ki finger** can be viewed as a reduced application of live hand because it is obviously impossible to grab someone's wrist with an open hand. This energetic aspect refers to the extension of the index finger while grabbing the attacker, shaking hands or executing certain joint locks.

• **Sunbayuk** is the energetic aspect of the principle of using the hips as the delivery systems of a person's power. Here, it refers primarily to the proper distribution of ki to assist physical force, enhance balance and facilitate circular movements. There is a difference between *sunbayuk* and the principle in body mechanics, but it is too subtle and difficult to put into words. In the body mechanics principle, I am talking about the importance of the hips strictly as an anatomical, physical structure. Sunbayuk is an Eastern concept referring to the channeling of ki energy through the hips.

• **Flinch reflex** is a well-known response of the autonomic nervous system that causes a person to be startled into disorganized and ineffective movement in a sudden attack. The combat-hapkido practitioner uses this instinctive reaction to his advantage. Through practice, he learns to react with a slightly modified version of this naturally occurring autonomic response. The modifications lie in the structurally defensive organization of the movement and the instinctive use of ki. The unique, simple defensive stance is a static illustration of the flinch reflex. When a person perceives the beginning of a verbal or physical confrontation, this stance is assumed, and when the attack comes, the flinch reflex makes the same posture dynamic and more energetic. Another way to look at this concept is that instead of constructing a slow, complex, artificial motor skill to respond to a sudden attack (such as with traditional blocks), you simply utilize a slightly improved version of an already existing, fast, natural motor skill. This concept, further refined, later results in a blending of defense and attack, wherein they become one and the same.

As you have seen, the difference between body mechanics and energetic principles is a fine and sometimes blurred line, each principle manifesting aspects of both. Effective physical movements require proper energy direction and utilization. That's what makes martial arts techniques so special.

Tactical Concepts

Physical confrontations do not occur in a sterile vacuum. They are events that combine many dynamic components, some existing in the environment, and others generated (intentionally or not) by the participants. That is also why the "one size fits all" approach to self-defense falls woefully short in the real world outside the controlled environment of the dojang. As a simple illustration of this, consider where a confrontation may take place. The attack (and the defense) can happen on a sidewalk, on a sandy beach, on rocky and uneven ground, on grass, on a stairwell, in a crowded club, in an airplane, on the bleachers of a stadium, in the rain, on icy ground, in an elevator, while sitting in a vehicle, while lying in bed, etc. As you can see from this brief list, terrain, locale, weather conditions, clothing, the presence of other people, availability of improvised weapons and escape routes make for a staggering variety of possibilities. Any of those factors, or a combination of them, will have an effect on the outcome of physical combat.

Tactical concepts involve the correct analysis of the situation and selection of the appropriate response. To understand the importance of this, look at the following scenario: In a traditional martial arts class, a group of students is drilled in throwing a reverse punch. Many repetitions are performed, and everyone in the class is expected to develop speed, power and accuracy. But no consideration is given to the inconvenient fact that a 100-pound woman punching a 200-pound man will most likely cause no serious damage other than to her own hand. Contrary to what many martial arts instructors proclaim, size, age, gender and level of fitness are important and play a vital role in any physical confrontation. The inclusion of tactical concepts is what is needed and is often lacking in self-defense training. They are the difference between just knowing how to execute a mechanically correct punch and knowing when, where, whom and whether to punch.

The following are some concepts and principles that will enhance your ability to make tactical decisions:

- **The PEDA principle** refers to a universal neurological four-step process that the brain always engages when confronted with a threat. The P stands for "perception," which is the function of the brain becoming aware of sound, movement or other external activity/input. The E stands for "evaluation," which is the analysis of what was perceived: Is it dangerous or harmless? The D stands for "decision," in which you select the appropriate response. From your decision, you come to A, or "action." You are now able to choose a dynamic, physical movement to deal with the situation.

  Depending on the individual, the environment and other conditions, the whole process may take as little as three-quarters of a second or up to several seconds. This, in extreme cases, may be the difference between life and death. Reality-based training must include a discussion of this process and practical drills (such as those in trapping) to speed up how fast your body and mind react to the PEDA principle. Note that the flinch-reflex and economy-of-movement concepts already reviewed are strongly connected to the physical aspect of the PEDA principle.

- **Distraction** is a practical concept that is unique to combat hapkido. The importance of this strategic element becomes obvious when training to execute a joint lock on a resisting partner. If your partner uses strong physical force to grab your wrist (or another part of your body or clothing), you won't be able to apply the joint lock. His tight and forceful grip won't allow you to maneuver your wrist to execute one. This is when distraction is vital. By first striking (even lightly) a sensitive part of the attacker's anatomy, you create a threat, causing the inevitable PEDA process to take place in your attacker's brain. On a physical level, you simply force him to go through an autonomic response to the pain. This causes the grab to be loosened because his brain is now obligated to deal with the effect of the strike. He is distracted, although temporarily, from his original intent. The loosened grip and the diverted focus provide the time and opportunity for you to apply the joint lock.

- **The high-and-low principle** takes advantage of predictable autonomic responses to give you the upper hand in a fight. It is a strategically smart and extremely effective way to deliver multiple strikes to unprotected areas. As an illustration, let's create a scenario in which the attacker is closing the gap and is ready to punch you. You swiftly go through the PEDA process and choose to deliver a low kick to the unprotected shinbone of the attacker. In doing so, you cause him to experience an autonomic response to pain; he lowers his hands and slightly bends forward at the head and torso. This drops his defense of vulnerable areas, so you can now strike high at his unprotected head. This again causes an autonomic response but in the opposite direction—his hands will come up, and the head and torso will bend backward. The attacker will leave his lower body exposed and unprotected.

  In combat hapkido, students are taught not to deliver a barrage of strikes to the same area because the attacker will inevitably immediately cover and protect that area, and his brain, through the PEDA process, will decide how to best deal with the situation. The high-and-low principle is a tool that confuses the brain and manipulates the attacker's body into predictable positions, giving you an invaluable advantage.

- **Vulnerable anatomy** is a concept that is common to all martial arts. It posits that striking or manipulating the most vulnerable parts of the body—eyes, nose, throat, groin, shins, etc.—will produce the fastest and most devastating results. The bad news is that the attacker will know this, too, and will endeavor to protect and not to expose those areas.

  Combat hapkido always implicitly assumes that the attacker is no dummy and that he has a basic understanding of the human body. That is why the selection of very vulnerable targets is inextricably connected to the two previously discussed principles: distraction and high-and-low. One of the functions of those two principles is to provide easy access to the most desirable targets.

At this point, on the subject, you need to consider another important issue. As in the proverbial *yin* and *yang*, attacking the most vulnerable areas allows smaller, weaker, older or younger defenders to inflict a great amount of pain on their attacker. This helps them stop an assault or secure an escape. On the negative side, you must understand that striking those vulnerable areas with enough force may cause serious permanent injury or even death to the attacker. This reality cannot be lightly dismissed or understated. It must be present in the cognitive process of every martial artist, and it must be explained to students during training so they do not develop a reckless, anything-goes mind-set. Obviously, when one's life is in danger, using whatever force is necessary to protect it—even with deadly results—is morally, ethically and legally acceptable. You must remember, however, that especially in those extreme cases, the burden of proof that excessive or wanton force was not used will rest with you. This is another reason combat hapkido is an extremely versatile system. Its principles give you options as to the degree of force you can use in any given situation.

- **Redundancy** is a concept that refers to how a technique should work even if you miss the target or your attacker isn't responding to it. A good example of redundancy is in the use of pressure points. The existence of pressure points in the human body is an accepted fact and has been known for centuries by practitioners of Asian martial arts. It is also known that some individuals are nonrespondent or only partially respondent to techniques that attack those points. Add to this the effect of drugs, alcohol, heavy clothing and other factors, and it becomes evident that dependence on pressure points in self-defense can be a costly mistake. They just aren't always 100 percent guaranteed to give you the advantage in a fight. That's why while many strikes, kicks and joint locks do in fact target one or more pressure points, combat hapkido teaches students that the points they target must be easy to locate, simple to activate and, most important, non-critical to the success of the technique. The pressure point is viewed as a desirable and effective enhancement of a technique but not as an indispensable or even a necessary element of it.

- **Speed**, of all the concepts, principles and physical attributes of self-defense, is the most important. As already mentioned in economy of movement, flinch reflex and PEDA, the goal in combat hapkido is to cut down the response time to an attack. In fact, I affirm that all those principles exist primarily and precisely to achieve the ultimate objective: speed. In a close-quarters attack, it is better to be fast than to be strong. The difference is between being hit by that first punch—maybe the only one needed to take you out—or successfully deflecting it and countering with a lightning-fast technique. Speed can be substantially improved simply by training for it. Relaxed repetitions of a technique initially serve to learn its mechanical movements, called "muscle memory." Once that is accomplished, many additional repetitions at a faster and faster tempo will dramatically increase your speed, and that will greatly improve the odds of your survival.

The Warrior Mind-Set

Self-defense includes basic and obvious principles such as awareness, prevention and avoidance. These preventatives have been taught and discussed at length by many personal-protection experts, security and law-enforcement agencies, and even the media for as long as crime has been a concern of society. Locking the doors of your house and car, not walking alone at night, not visiting a bar in a rough neighborhood, not flashing money or jewelry, and not getting intoxicated at a party are all sound and timeless advice for living a safer life anywhere in the world. The ability to talk yourself out of a bad situation is also a smart and recommended course of action.

But the warrior mind-set goes way beyond that. Awareness and readiness alone will not always be enough in a fight. Likewise, just because you train in a self-defensive martial art doesn't mean you are guaranteed to succeed in the face of danger. This is when the core of the warrior mind-set comes in. It is not just about the ability to be aware and ready to fight or to have the ability and skill to fight. It is about the will to do so.

This is not as cut and dry as it seems, and contrary to what many believe, it is not true that some people have it and others don't. The truth is that most human beings will be affected differently by many specific factors at different times and will react accordingly. It has been demonstrated that under certain stressful and dangerous conditions, a tough guy may crumble, while a normally meek or passive individual may react with the fury of a tiger. This is often observed when everyday people are faced with mortal danger or catastrophic events. They become unlikely heroes and perform deeds of incredible courage, strength, daring and sacrifice. Anyone familiar with troops in combat can also attest to this and will tell you that the soldier with the warrior mind-set does not always look or act like Rambo.

Potentially, everyone can develop a warrior ethos, but in reality, only a small minority of people do develop it. The reasons for that are many and complex: family upbringing, peer influence, genetic makeup, philosophical and religious beliefs, social conditioning, etc. So the bottom line of all this is that just because someone is a student of the martial arts doesn't mean he will rise to the challenge and fight back when attacked. Of course, all things equal, it is always better to have self-defense training and skills than not. They can certainly help and might reduce the damage. But the unwavering will and determination to fight back and survive are indispensable ingredients of a successful outcome.

The warrior mind-set naturally includes elements of courage, commitment, moral imperative and righteous justice. It also contains a little-understood element of great strategic value that is much harder to neatly define. It can be called "calmness of mind." This is an emotional and intellectual state wherein the individual facing the threat or danger remains calm. In fact, the individual not only remains calm but also is able to instantly silence, or at least ignore, the disrupting background noise of passions, fears, preconceived judgments and other distracting concerns. That person is then capable of focusing completely and absolutely on the task at hand. In the case of a combat-hapkido practitioner, he is able to face the threat and effectively synthesize the concepts in this chapter with his technical training.

Some Japanese martial arts have a very specific term for this aspect of the warrior mind-set: *mushin*. Like many other Eastern conceptual words, it is probably impossible to translate exactly, but the closest approximation is "the mind of no mind." What the definition conveys is the somewhat abstract concept of not letting your ordinary, everyday thinking process interfere with and negatively affect the necessary, uncluttered calmness of mind and spirit required for lightning-fast appropriate physical action in combat. To illustrate mushin at work, let's look at the following simple example:

A visibly larger and stronger opponent who is ready to initiate a physical confrontation approaches you. Instead of calmly focusing on the best course of action—avoidance, escape, selection of targets, most effective technique, etc.—your mind is busy or overwhelmed by thoughts. You may be thinking things such as, He is so big … He is too strong … He will hurt me … I can wind up in the hospital seriously injured … My technique will not work on this guy … I should not have come here … etc. You get the picture. This is much more than lack of confidence or normal and natural fear. It is the debilitating confusion of emotions and preconceived notions clouding your mind, sapping your spirit and possibly paralyzing your body.

Under those conditions, fast, decisive and accurate responses are extremely difficult to employ even if you have the technical knowledge. On the other hand, someone who has made mushin an integral part of his warrior mind-set will instantly banish those detrimental thoughts from the mind. Ideally, at the most advanced levels, the warrior will not even have to do that; he will no longer consciously experience that process.

It is also vital to understand that mushin is neutral and works both ways. In a situation opposite to the one already described, say you are confronted by a smaller, weaker-looking individual. Now the thoughts clouding your judgment may sound something like this: "Oh, he is so small … He looks like a wimp … I could easily kick his butt … I will teach him a lesson … etc." The concept of mushin teaches that those thoughts are just as damaging, undesirable and even dangerous.

Simply put, do not ever overestimate or underestimate the threat. Do not be overly confident or lack confidence entirely. The warrior mind-set requires an analytical mind that calmly assesses the situation in realistic, not emotional, terms. It helps you take into account equally all factors (yes, including the size of your opponent) and instantly formulate the proper response, drawing on your internal energy, experience, skills and unshakable resolve.

When mushin becomes part of your overall warrior spirit, you will have many strategic and tactical advantages. Your calm, focused mind will quickly anticipate attacks, find escape routes, suggest the right verbal persuasion, discover available improvised weapons, select the most vulnerable targets, choose the best technique, and ultimately help you resolve the confrontation in your favor with the least amount of violence possible and without devastating legal consequences.

CHAPTER 5
STRIKING AND KICKING

There are no special, defining characteristics of kicks or strikes in combat hapkido. A kick is a kick is a kick, and in self-defense, speed and hitting the target are really all that matter. Turning a kick into a scientific dissertation about pivoting, hip rotation, curling of toes, locking versus unlocking the knee, etc. is something that traditional or sport-based martial artists can indulge in because they are practiced in controlled environments.

Instead, combat-hapkido strikes and kicks are characterized by the principles and concepts discussed in Chapter 4. Like any martial art, combat-hapkido strikes and kicking, even with the principles and concepts, cannot absolutely guarantee victory in a fight. No one has all the answers for all possible situations, and ultimately, it is not solely the art or style that counts. It is the individual and his level of skill, fitness, determination and warrior mind-set that give him the best chance at success.

Strikes

There are some general guidelines, however, that combat hapkido applies to strikes. You will use redirection, deflection, trapping and checking to set up a strike. Students are also encouraged to always strike at the face and head area. The reason is that area contains the computer of the human body. You want to rattle and stun the computer and also affect the visual field. In addition to distracting and stunning an attacker—to follow up with a joint lock or takedown maneuver—strikes are also used as power techniques to stop the attacker in his tracks. How you decide depends on the distance (range), the size of attacker, the environment, your abilities, the legal ramifications, etc.

Open-hand strikes are favored for several practical reasons. First, unlike hard punches, they prevent possible damage to the hand. Second, the open hand can instantly transition from trapping to striking to joint locking without requiring major biomechanical or energetic changes. Finally, punching requires power to do damage. A 90-pound woman will have little effect punching a 200-pound man, so will a child punching an adult. Instead, open-hand strikes rely on speed and accuracy, targeting areas that cause damage or pain with little power.

Eye Jab

This is an open-hand strike that uses the *ki*-energized and extended fingers to jab the attacker's eyes.

Ki Slap

The *ki* slap is another open-hand strike. Unlike the eye jab, it uses the back of the hand to attack the face or soft-tissue targets—such as the solar plexus, kidneys or groin—of the body. Note how it also uses live hand and ki finger to energize the strike.

Palm Heel

The palm heel is an open-hand strike that uses the hard, bottom inside of the hand to attack bone structures on the face or the torso (such as the sternum or floating ribs).

Tiger Mouth

1-2. Using the connective tissues between the thumb and index finger, this open-hand strike is directed almost exclusively to the attacker's throat. Also note how the *ki* finger is present in both hands when executing the strike.

Sudo

Popularly known as the karate chop, this open-hand strike uses the outside bottom edge of the hand. Depending on the energy and power generated, it can be used to attack soft-tissue targets (such as the throat) or bone structures (such as the collarbone).

Note: All fighting systems contain punching techniques, and although combat hapkido favors open-hand strikes, the system also includes selected punches for specific situations for those individuals who can generate enough power to make them effective.

Vertical Punch

1-3. Popularized by Bruce Lee, this is a linear, close-quarters, no-chambering punch that relies on speed and energy as opposed to gross-muscular power. It can be used against most areas of the body. In these pictures, power delivery by the hips is quite obvious.

Backfist Punch

1-2. Common to most martial arts, this semicircular strike uses the back of the hand to hit hard and soft targets of the head and torso.

Hammerfist

1-2. This punch uses the same outside bottom part of the hand as the *sudo* strike but with a closed fist. It can be effectively delivered vertically downward, such as on the bridge of the nose or clavicle, or horizontally, such as to the solar plexus or rib cage.

Ulnar Strike

1-2. Known also as a forearm strike, this close-quarters technique uses the middle of the ulnar bone to deliver great power on impact. It is best to keep the hand open with extended *ki*-finger energy. It can be used for many targets, but it is especially effective against the soft tissues of the neck, wherein hard bone hits nerves and blood vessels.

Elbow Strike

1-3. At very close quarters, elbows are valuable defensive weapons and, albeit somewhat overrated, are included in most martial arts training. The elbow can be used as a spear by using the tip against the face of the charging attacker.

4-6. It can also be used as a bar by using the ulnar bone to hit the head or torso.

Kicks

Unlike most traditional or sport-based martial arts, kicks in combat hapkido are delivered primarily to the lower body because they are more effective and easier to execute in an adrenaline-filled situation than high, acrobatic kicks. As with combat hapkido strikes, they can be used to distract or stun an attacker, setting him up for a follow-up technique. They can also be used to stop an advancing attacker or as a finishing technique to take him to the ground.

The following are other reasons to avoid high kicks in a real fight:

- They leave the kicker vulnerable and off-balance (on one leg) too long.

- They take longer to reach the target, giving the attacker time to potentially block them or absorb them with his arms.

- Low kicks targeting the legs of the attacker cannot be blocked, and if powerful enough, they will take away the attacker's mobility.

Front Kick

1-2. Preferably delivered with the lead leg (closest to the attacker), the linear front kick uses the ball of the foot or, when wearing strong shoes, the toes. It is directed to the shins, knees, thighs, groin or lower abdomen.

3. It's also possible to attack with the rear leg or to target either the opponent's lead or rear leg.

Side Kick

1-4. Using the outer blade of the foot, this linear kick can be delivered to the upper part of the lower body, to the middle of the leg or at knee level.

Roundhouse Kick

1-2. This circular kick can use the tip of the foot (with strong shoes), the instep or even the shinbone according to the distance between you and the attacker. It is directed to the outside or inside of the attacker's upper leg, depending on which leg is forward.

Back Kick

1-3. A linear kick using the whole foot directed to the groin or abdomen of an attacker who is grabbing or approaching from behind.

Scoop Kick

1-4. This semicircular kick uses the inside edge of the foot and is always targeted at the knees or shins of the attacker to off-balance him. This is a very close-quarters kick best employed during a grappling or clinching situation. Notice that in all the pictures, the hands are executing a joint lock or takedown maneuver while the feet are kicking.

Knee Kicks

1-6. Like the elbows, knees can be a very effective defensive weapon but only at very close range (mostly grappling). Knee strikes can be vertical (upward) or diagonal. They can be used against the attacker's upper leg (inside or outside) or even to the torso or head, provided they have been lowered within reach.

Striking and kicking techniques are common to all fighting arts. Each style does it just a little differently. Combat hapkido contains a good arsenal of strikes and kicks but one that is not too extensive, complex, flashy or difficult to execute. Fancy acrobatic techniques have no place in reality-based self-defense and can, in fact, be dangerous to your health. And while all training should be done and is best done with a partner while under the direction of a qualified instructor, striking and kicking are two things that you can practice by yourself, even at home, by simply using a heavy bag or a martial arts dummy. Many repetitions will develop speed, stamina, accuracy and power.

CHAPTER 6
CLOSING THE GAP WITH TRAPPING

In combat hapkido, it all starts with the system's lack of formal stances. From a simple, relaxed defensive posture with open hands, it is easy and efficient and makes more sense biomechanically to trap than to try to hard-block, which is a tense, slower, less economic movement and possibly damaging to the limbs of the defender. That's why combat hapkido practitioners trap—which, by the way, is a catch-all word for deflecting, parrying, checking, swatting, passing, brushing, etc.

Blocking vs. Trapping

1-2. When the defender blocks, he is trying to defeat his attacker with pure power. He also exposes himself to the opponent's counterattacks. When he traps, he manipulates the attacker's movement and strength to work against him. He also moves fluidly from defense to offense.

There are virtually hundreds of trapping and counter-trapping sequences, drills and exercises that can be practiced (one of the most famous being *chi sao*, or sticky hands, of the Chinese art of wing chun). Out of that vast body of knowledge, I selected only a small portion of trapping concepts and techniques for inclusion in the combat-hapkido curriculum. The criteria used for choosing the correct ones were that they had to blend and integrate smoothly with the style's techniques, they had to be reasonably easy to learn, and they had to enhance the system's techniques without requiring mechanical changes.

The addition of trapping to combat-hapkido training has been one of the most important elements in the evolution of the system, increasing the speed of counterstrikes and facilitating the application of joint locks. It is most useful and effective against linear attacks (such as a jab or a cross) but can also be used against circular attacks (such as a hook punch). In all cases, it protects you, helps you close the gap and allows you to quickly take control of the attacker. The following are some of combat hapkido's most commonly used trapping techniques and encountered scenarios:

Brush-Trap Strike

1. The attacker (right) prepares to throw a jab.

2. The defender displaces the punching arm by slightly deflecting it with an open lead hand.

3. He traps the punching hand, grabbing the attacker's right wrist cross-hand and pulling it to his midsection.

4. The defender finishes the attacker with a strike—in this case a *ki* slap—to the attacker's face. The defender could also have executed an eye jab.

Cross-Brush-Trap Strike

1. The attacker and defender (left) face each other in a cross stance. The attacker prepares to throw a jab at the defender.

2. The defender slightly deflects the punching arm with his open lead hand.

3. With speed, the defender traps the attacker's elbow against his own body with the rear hand.

4. This tactical and quick move gives the defender enough time to deliver a high forearm strike to the attacker's exposed neck. Note how the defender still maintains a check on the trapped elbow.

Split-Entry Trap Strike

1. The attacker (left) prepares to throw a jab.

2. The defender moves his head slightly outside of the line of attack while checking the punching arm with his open lead hand.

3. On the inside line, the defender delivers an eye jab.

Inside-the-Guard Trap Strike

1. The attacker throws a hook punch, which the defender appears to block. It is like a block, but in effect, it traps the arm, becoming a double strike. The principle at play here is the water principle, clearly penetrating the attack. The defense and the counter are one and the same.

2-3. It's actually a check for just inside the punching arm. The rear forearm disrupts the attacker's movement, while the lead forearm strikes at the attacker's neck.

Raised-Shield Trap Strike

1. The attacker throws a hook punch off of the defender's centerline. The defender intercepts it with his lead outside upper arm.

2. By disrupting the punch, the defender can immediately flow into and deliver a lead open-hand strike to the attacker's face and execute a trap.

3. He then strikes low with an upward palm strike to the groin.

4. Because the target is a vulnerable area of anatomy, the attacker bends forward in pain, allowing the defender to finish him with an upward knee strike to the face.

Foot Trapping

Another element that I to added to combat hapkido is what I call "foot trapping." It is not related to hand trapping, and it is totally independent of it. I became interested in foot trapping during training with Willem de Thouars, one of the world's leading experts on *kun tao silat* (a blend of Indonesian and Chinese fighting styles). The footwork, leg attacks and foot traps of that system are primarily designed to disrupt the balance and restrict the mobility of the attacker. Once again, I had no intention to bring a whole other art into the combat-hapkido system; I just wanted to introduce a few simple and effective foot movements to assist students with their joint locks and takedowns. But that is the advantage an eclectic style has over a traditional one: the freedom to include useful elements from other arts to improve the overall effectiveness of the system.

In combat hapkido, foot trapping is not mandated or necessary in every technique. It is just a helpful, optional addition to facilitate, enhance or assist a technique in progress. In the following two examples, you'll notice that the foot traps are subtle, close-quarters attributes of footwork used to restrict the attacker's movement, disrupt his balance, facilitate takedowns and, at times, enhance joint-locking techniques. Consistent with the concept of economy of movement, foot trapping in combat hapkido also replaces the leg-sweeping of traditional martial arts.

Cross Inside Foot Trap

1. The defender (right) grapples with an attacker.

2. He lowers his center of gravity to increase his body's stability. At the same time, he brings his right foot inside and around the attacker's right foot, restricting the attacker's motion.

3. Bending the right knee, the defender takes the attacker down by disrupting his balance.

Same-Side Outside Foot Trap

1. The attacker grabs the defender's shoulder and prepares to punch.

2. Because of his training, the defender goes rapidly through the PEDA process. He makes a tactical decision and acts by raising his arms to protect his head while lowering his center of gravity. At the same time, he brings his left foot around the attacker's lead foot, trapping it.

3. The defender pushes down with his shinbone against the attacker's leg.

4. This disrupts the attacker's balance, restricts his motion and takes him down.

Combat hapkido uses "trapping" as a big-tent word. Underneath it, the student will find many subtle variations, differences and combinations: traps that are almost like blocks but function as strikes; checks that lead to grabs and locks; parries that accomplish deflections; footwork that results in balance disruption; and foot traps that immobilize lower joints to facilitate takedowns. It is all connected. And although this may appear complicated, it is actually fairly easy to learn and extremely effective in a real fight. In fact, when the principles the student has already covered—such as the flinch reflex, economy of movement and speed—are incorporated in the body mechanics of trapping, the student will find the techniques natural, efficient and flowing smoothly.

CHAPTER 7
DEFENSE AGAINST GRABS AND CHOKES

Because some form of grabbing is almost always present during a fight—at the beginning, in the middle or at the end—combat hapkido teaches a great variety of defenses and counters not only to respond to the grab but also, in many cases, to take advantage of the fact that you are being grabbed. It welcomes the grab as an opportunity to employ specifically designed techniques.

Combat hapkido groups grabs into several categories, which include wrist grabs, chest grabs, shoulder grabs, garment grabs, bear hugs, breakaways, etc. These categories are further subdivided into one-hand grabs, two-hand grabs, grabs from the front, grabs from the side, grabs from behind, etc. With this teaching methodology, students learn to defend against almost all possible scenarios and even some unlikely ones.

At this point, I want to remind readers that several of the underlying principles will be generally present in most of these techniques dealing with grabs. For example, when someone (especially someone larger and stronger than you) grabs your wrist, it is futile and ineffective to try to forcefully pull away because trying to do so ignores and violates the three main principles of hapkido (water, circular and harmony). Instead, by remembering the simple formula "When pushed, pull; when pulled, push," you will be instinctively incorporating them into your response. So when an attacker grabs your wrist to pull you, push your arm toward him (penetrating the attack like water). At the same time, redirect his pull in a slightly circular motion (thus affecting his balance and energy), and by not trying to pull away as in a tug of war, you are not meeting force with force (harmony).

Other subtle benefits accrue when you follow these principles: Your attacker will be surprised because you are doing the opposite of what he expects. That will unfavorably affect his PEDA process, resulting in indecision and him possibly taking the wrong reaction. All this may be a little hard to internalize when reading or too subtle to detect in photo sequences, but during actual training, the concepts and their applications are quite easy to absorb.

Before you move on, two more reminders need to be made: First, all the techniques shown are what we call "mirror-reversible," meaning that they work exactly the same on both sides, right or left. Second, that breakaways (escapes or releases) are not trying to take advantage of the grab through joint manipulations or to counter-grab the attacker to place him into a painful lock. Instead, you are simply breaking contact by escaping from the grab to follow up with a strike or kick, or to just walk away from a nonthreatening situation. During the study of combat hapkido, breakaways are one of the first things that students learn because they're easy and they give students confidence. While all grabs are potentially dangerous, not all of them require a forceful response or the immobilization of the person doing the grabbing. Legal and tactical considerations will govern your decision in accordance with your PEDA process. Further picture sequences will illustrate appropriate responses in more threatening situations.

Same-Side Breakaway

1. The attacker grabs the defender's left wrist with his right hand (same side).

2. Using the live-hand concept, the defender keeps his caught hand open with his fingers extended and bends his elbow forward.

3. He frees his wrist by energetically shooting his arm back toward himself.

4. If warranted, the defender follows up with a face strike.

Cross-Wrist Breakaway

1. The attacker grabs the defender's right wrist with his right hand (cross-hand).

2. Keeping his right hand open and live, the defender delivers a *sudo* strike to the radial nerve of the attacker's right wrist.

3. The pain of the strike causes the attacker to let go, freeing the defender.

Two-Hand Breakaway

1. The attacker grabs both the defender's wrists.

2. Keeping both his hands open and live, the defender lowers one hand with the palm down while raising the other with the palm up.

3. With speed and energy, the defender smashes the back of the attacker's hands against each other.

4. The impact should cause the attacker to open his grip or loosen his grip, allowing the defender to free the upper hand.

Continued ➡

5. Considering the economy of movement, the defender uses his action to free his hand to immediately deliver a face strike.

Defense Against Same-Side Wrist Grab, No. 1

1. The attacker grabs the defender's left wrist with his right hand.

2. The defender delivers a fast, low-line kick to the attacker's shin to loosen his grip and distract him.

3. He counter-grabs the attacker's right wrist with his left hand.

4. He then grabs the attacker's hand with his own right hand.

5. The defender then applies a painful joint lock by torquing the trapped hand toward the attacker.

Defense Against Same-Side Wrist Grab, No. 2

1. The attacker grabs the defender's left wrist with his right hand.

2. The defender counters with a quick eye jab.

3-4. He then brings his right hand behind the attacker's right elbow to pull it forward. As always, when grabbed, the defender's hand goes live with *ki* energy.

5. The defender pulls the attacker as far forward as possible to free his trapped hand.

6-9. The defender then inserts his arm inside the attacker's. This pulls the attacker in and locks his arm and shoulder, which allows the defender to take him to the ground.

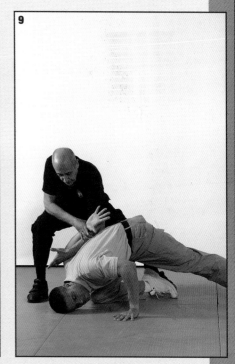

Defense Against Same-Side Wrist Grab, No. 3

1. The attacker grabs the defender's left wrist with his right hand.

2. The defender kicks the attacker's shin with his front leg to prevent the attacker from launching a punch.

3. To off-balance the attacker, the defender pulls his trapped left arm toward himself.

4. He quickly switches hands. He grabs the attacker's right wrist with his right hand while freeing the trapped left hand.

5. Taking into account economy of movement, the defender delivers an elbow strike to the attacker's face.

6. The defender then grabs the attacker's hand with both his own.

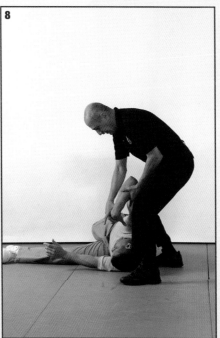

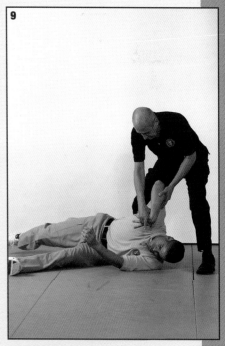

7-9. He torques the attacker's arm, taking him to the ground in a counterclockwise motion. If he chooses, the defender can maintain control with a wrist lock.

Defense Against Same-Side Wrist Grab, No. 4

1. When the attacker grabs the defender's wrist, the defender retaliates this time with a low side kick to his knee.

2. He pulls the attacker toward him while grabbing the attacker's right wrist. This frees the defender's left hand.

3. Next, the defender reaches under the attacker's arm.

4. He grabs the attacker's fingers.

5. By bending the attacker's trapped fingers back, the defender causes his opponent a lot of pain, which also controls him. He also creates space by stepping away from the attacker.

Defense Against Cross-Wrist Grab, No. 1

1. When grabbed on the right wrist by the attacker's right hand, the defender immediately distracts the attacker by kicking his leg.

2. He brings his right hand up while grabbing the attacker's wrist with his left hand.

Continued ➡

3. He frees his right hand.

4-6. Torquing the attacker's hand with both his own, the defender executes a takedown. He widens his base to do so.

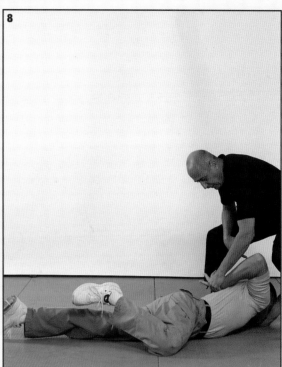

7-8. The defender maintains control of the attacker by turning him over and continuing the application of a joint lock.

Defense Against Cross-Wrist Grab, No. 2

1. The attacker grabs the defender's right wrist.

2. The defender kicks the attacker's leg.

Continued ▶

3. Rotating his right hand clockwise, the defender counter-grabs the attacker's wrist.

4. The defender applies an armbar by pressing his left forearm (ulna bone) against the attacker's right triceps. Note the *ki* finger and live hand.

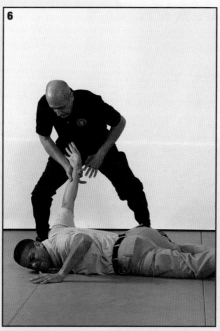

5. He then takes the attacker down.

6-7. The defender can maintain control if he needs to with the arm lock.

Defense Against Cross-Wrist Grab, No. 3

1. In this scenario, the defender pulls the attacker toward him while counter-grabbing the attacker's right wrist.

2. Stepping behind the attacker with his left leg, the defender reaches around to grip the attacker's neck with his left hand.

3. By gripping the attacker's trachea and twisting the attacker's head, the defender locks his opponent against him.

Defense Against Cross-Wrist Grab, No. 4

1. Against a cross-wrist attack, the defender kicks the attacker in the groin area.

2. After the low counter, the defender rotates his arm clockwise to off-balance the opponent.

3. He grabs the attacker's hand with both his hands.

4. He then controls him with a painful joint lock by torquing his hand toward the left.

5. From here, the defender can also take the attacker to the ground.

Defense Against Two-Handed Grab (Front)

1. The attacker grabs both the defender's wrists from the front.

2. Like in a single-hand grab, the defender kicks the attacker to loosen up his grip.

3. The defender counter-grabs both the attacker's wrists.

4-5. He raises one hand high.

Continued →

6-7. At the same time, he steps across and in front of the attacker.

8-9. This causes the attacker's arms to pass over the defender's head and cross.

10-12. From here, the defender can take his opponent to the ground.

Defense Against Two-Handed Grab (Rear)

1-2. In this attack, the defender immediately widens his base and feigns an attempt to escape on one side.

3. He suddenly switches sides and raises his right arm over his head. This off-balances the attacker.

4. Continuing with his motion, the defender steps backward completely. This also puts him across and behind the attacker.

5. He can also use his trapped left hand to free his trapped right wrist by grabbing the attacker's raised wrist.

6. Now the defender can completely free himself by torquing the attacker's wrist in and downward.

7. If needed, the defender can follow up with a kick to the attacker's face.

8. He can also take his opponent to the ground.

Defense Against One-Handed Chest Grab, No. 1

1. The attacker grabs the defender's shirt with his right hand.

2. As a distraction, the defender shoots his right hand to the attacker's face.

3. Simultaneously, he pushes the attacker's elbow across the attacker's body.

4. The defender snakes his right arm under the attacker's right and strikes the attacker's face to rotate his opponent's head toward his left side.

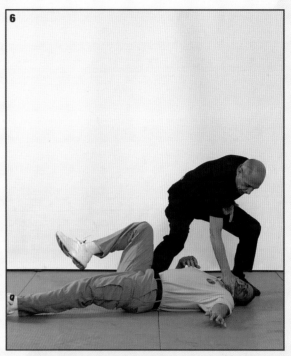

5. The defender continues the pressure.

6-7. The defender takes the attacker down, and if needed, he follows up with strikes to anywhere vulnerable and easily accessible.

Defense Against One-Handed Chest Grab, No. 2

1. The attacker grabs the defender's clothes with his left hand while making threatening gestures with his right index finger extended.

2. Using his left hand, the defender grabs the attacker's index finger while stepping back with his left leg to widen his base.

3. He applies a painful finger lock by bending it back toward the attacker and down. From here, the defender can also take the attacker to the ground.

Defense Against One-Handed Chest Grab, No. 3

1. When the attacker grabs the defender's shirt, the defender immediately delivers a horizontal strike with his forearm to the attacker's right wrist. The defender torques his hips for maximum power.

2. He torques his hips again to deliver a face strike with his left hand, completing freeing himself from the attacker's grip.

Defense Against Two-Handed Chest Grab

1. The attacker grabs the defender's shirt with both hands.

2. The defender shoots one hand into the attacker's face to cause a reaction.

3. Then the defender flows with his body to wrap his arm over and around the attacker's other arm. The leverage generated by this movement causes the attacker to lose his grip.

4-6. Having released himself from the grabs, the defender applies a joint lock.

7. From there, the defender can take the attacker to the ground by continuously applying pressure.

Defense Against One-Handed Shoulder Grab (Front or Side)

1. It doesn't matter whether the attacker grabs the defender's shoulder from the front or side. The defender reacts by using his open hand to strike the side of the attacker's face on the same side of the grab.

2. While doing this, the defender also traps the grabbing hand with his free right hand.

3. He wraps his striking arm over and around the attacker's grabbing arm.

4. Then the defender pulls the attacker's arm close to his chest while widening his base.

5. When the defender takes the attacker to the ground, he can maintain control with an armbar or lock.

Defense Against One-Handed Shoulder Grab (Rear), No. 1

1. The defender is surprised by a shoulder grab from behind.

2. He steps back to the side of the attacker with his arm raised. The defender in this case steps in the direction of the grab (i.e., right shoulder grab, step to the right).

Continued ➡

3. Continuing the arm movement, the defender is naturally able to strike at the attacker's face.

4. Pivoting his body, the defender continues through with the motion of the strike to grab at the attacker's right wrist. He also strikes the attacker's face again with his left hand. Note how the motion is very circular.

5. The defender pulls the attacker's captured arm to execute and finish his opponent with an armbar.

Defense Against One-Handed Shoulder Grab (Rear), No. 2

1. The defender is once again surprised by a shoulder grab from the rear, but this time, he happens to turn inside of the attacker's guard.

2-3. As he turns, the defender strikes the attacker's face with his lead hand.

Continued ➤

4-5. He continues the movement of his lead arm. This brings the defender's arm over and around the attacker's grabbing arm. The defender also strikes the attacker's face with his right hand. Note how circular the motion is.

6-7. When delivering the second strike, the defender steps behind the attacker's closest leg to apply a leg trap to execute a takedown.

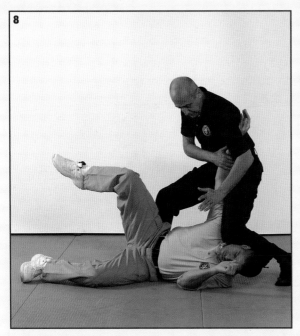

8-9. The defender can maintain control with an armbar.

Defense Against Two-Handed Elbow Grab (Rear)

1. The attacker tries to immobilize the defender by grabbing him by the elbows from behind.

2. The defender spreads out his arms and widens his base.

Continued ➤

3. The defender brings his left leg across and behind the attacker for a foot trap. He doesn't bring his right leg back.

4. While trapping the leg, the defender delivers an elbow strike to the already unbalanced attacker's stomach.

5. Using the pressure of his elbow and leg, the defender torques his hips to take the attacker down.

Defense Against Bear Hug, No. 1

1. The attacker clinches with a bear hug. The defender is surprised.

2. Quickly going through the PEDA process, the defender reacts by widening his base and bringing one hand in front of the attacker's face.

3. He pushes the attacker's head back to create space. Note that the defender places his index finger on the attacker's upper lip and at the base of the attacker's nose. If he pushes the attacker's head back with this pressure point, it will be easier to create space.

Continued ➤

4-6. Having exposed the attacker's neck, the defender drives his fingers down into the lower trachea. The attacker is forced to release his grip and go down.

Defense Against Bear Hug, No. 2

1. This time, the attacker comes from behind and traps the defender's arm tightly against his body.

2. The defender traps the attacker's two hands.

3. One hand holds the attacker's hand down (so he cannot pull away), while the other peels off one of the attacker's fingers. It does not matter which hand does what.

4. Keeping his opponent's hand against his body, the defender bends the attacker's finger until released.

Continued ➤

5. The defender spins free but maintains his finger lock.

6. He takes the attacker to the ground.

Chokes

Combat hapkido classifies chokes as the most extreme and dangerous form of grab because they can be fatal. An important point to remember is that all grabs are not created equal. What I mean is that unlike an attack beginning with a strike, in which the intent is obvious and not open to legal or moral interpretations, when contact initiates with a grab, it may not necessarily be dangerous or lead to an all-out fight. Although maybe annoying, unwelcome and rude, not all grabs demand a self-defense technique in response. This is why the PEDA process and warrior mind-set are so important. By considering them while training, you prepare yourself to make the best choices not only during a fight but also after it.

Defense Against Front Choke

1. The attacker attempts a frontal choke.

2. The defender makes a tactical decision and quickly brings both hands up to deliver a double open-hand strike to the attacker's ears.

Continued ➡

3. Before the attacker can react in surprise or pain, the defender then flows into his next movement—a trapping technique. He traps both of the attacker's hands under his crossed arms. This also loosens the attacker's chokehold.

4. By stepping back with one leg, the defender widens his base to force the attacker down.

5. Now the defender off-balances the attacker again by shooting his forearms out and into the attacker's face.

6. The attacker is thrown down and away from the defender.

Defense Against Rear Choke

1. The attacker applies a chokehold from behind.

2. The defender lifts his chin to create some space between his neck and the attacker's arm. Because time is a factor, he immediately thrusts his hands into the space just created.

3. The defender drops to a wide horse stance, pulling the attacker's arm down but tight on his own chest. The downward pull of the defender's arms against the attacker's arm creates the space needed to stop the choke.

4. Still holding his arm, the defender steps back and across with one leg behind the attacker. He steps on the side of the arm that is choking him and not vice versa. This movement helps the defender pull his head out from under the attacker's armpit and free from the choke.

Continued

5. Once free, the defender can further weaken the attacker with a shin or knee strike to the face.

6-7. He can also apply an arm lock (right to right or left to left, depending on which side escaped), apply downward pressure and take him to the ground.

CHAPTER 8
DEFENSE AGAINST PUNCHES AND KICKS

Many, if not most, unarmed violent confrontations, assaults and fights start with a single hand strike or kick. Unfortunately, what many people do not realize is that even a simple punch or kick delivered with enough force and connecting with a particularly vulnerable area can kill, maim or paralyze a human being. Sometimes, the punch will not cause the most serious injury but the fall resulting from it will. Police files around the world contain thousands of cases of individuals literally being beaten to death, sustaining brain damage, becoming disfigured or being rendered permanently disabled as a result of fights involving only hands and feet. A smart self-defense student should never brag, "I can take a punch," because it could be the fatal one. He should instead learn not to take one, ever!

In the real world, devastating damage will result in the individual not being able to counter, overcome, escape or, ultimately, survive. It is therefore imperative that instead of theatrical, prearranged sequences or glorified games of tag, instructors of reality-based martial arts teach their students how *not* to get hit. It is not as important to your health to know how to kick butt as it is to know how not to get your butt kicked!

This is why combat hapkido devotes a great portion of its training to defending against punches and kicks both in stand-up and ground-survival situations. Unlike boxers or UFC fighters (and in martial arts movies), the majority of people cannot sustain multiple powerful strikes to the body, especially the head and face, without serious injuries. Therefore, it is imperative that considerable training time be spent to learn how to avoid being hit by that first punch and to learn how to immediately counter and prevent additional punches being thrown against you. And because combat hapkido almost never employs hard blocks, the vital importance of trapping skills becomes evident. Trapping is the fastest and most natural initial defense against punches, and it is incorporated to different degrees in the dynamic attack responses you will see in this chapter.

Defenses Against Punches

In order to understand defenses against punches, you must first know how a punch is delivered. Fortunately, it is not complicated, and combat hapkido has further simplified the subject by using valuable and clear classifications. Punches are divided into two kinds: linear and circular. A jab and a cross are linear, while a hook (roundhouse) and an uppercut are circular. This simple boxing terminology is used because it is familiar to most people, even those who are not martial artists. During training, combat hapkido also covers other types of punches, such as backfists and hammerfists. It stresses, however, that while those are useful punches to learn and use, they are rarely employed by bad guys in a street fight or criminal attack. It is important to remember that in the real world, the self-defense practitioner will almost never have to confront the punches of a trained boxer or an expert martial artist. That's good news. The most common punches thrown in a street fight are the jab, cross and hook. The bad news is that even when thrown wildly by an untrained punk, they will do severe or even fatal damage if they connect with the right target and with enough power. So it cannot be overstated that this area of training is of the utmost importance.

Defense Against Jab

1. The attacker throws a jab to the defender's face. Using his open lead hand, the defender slightly deflects it.

2. He grabs the wrist of the attacker's punching hand with his rear hand, trapping it.

3. The defender strikes the attacker's face with his lead hand.

4-5. He then spins behind the attacker and delivers an elbow strike to his kidney area.

6. He follows up with a side kick to the back of the attacker's knee to take him down.

Split-Entry Defense Against Jab

1. The attacker throws a jab to the defender's face. The defender deflects it using his open lead hand.

2. With the rear hand, the defender delivers a finger jab to the attacker's eyes inside of his guard.

Continued ➤

3. He uses his striking hand to trap the attacker's punching arm.

4. The defender then applies an armbar.

5. The attacker is taken to the ground.

Defense Against Hook Punch, No. 1

1. The attacker throws a hook punch to the defender's head.

2-3. Shooting both his arms out with open hands, the defender strikes the punching forearm with one and the side of the attacker's neck with the other.

Continued ➡

4. He grabs the attacker's punching arm.

5. The defender wraps an arm over and around it.

6. Observe the wrap from the other side.

7. Bringing the attacker's arm to his chest, the defender locks it.

8. He uses his free hand to strike his opponent's face.

9. By pushing the attacker's head back, the defender can take him down.

Defense Against Hook Punch, No. 2

1. The attacker closes the gap.

2. He throws a hook punch to the defender's head, but the defender shoots both arms out with open hands, striking at the punching forearm and the side of the attacker's neck.

3-4. The defender grabs the punching arm and brings his other arm above the attacker's neck.

5-6. He pushes down on the back of his opponent's neck.

7-8. The defender wraps his arm around the attacker's neck.

Continued ➤

9-12. The defender applies a choke or a neck crank to the attacker.

Defenses Against Kicks

In combat hapkido, there are only two sensible ways to defend against a kick:

- If you have the room and the time, simply step back and let it miss.

- If you are too close or too late for the first option, close the gap by moving into the attacker's guard.

In other words, stay very far or very close. By depriving the attacker of the middle range needed to hit the target, you render his kick ineffective. Blocking kicks with your hands—especially low kicks—is unrealistic, and if attempted, it will result in injury to your arm and hand by the much bigger and stronger leg. Some martial arts instructors teach how to block or check kicks using your legs, which can work for strong, experienced fighters. However, because it presents too many risks—loss of balance, injury to the leg, etc.—this method is not included in combat hapkido.

Instead, combat hapkido prefers to neutralize the power of kicks by closing the gap (moving diagonally to very close-quarters range) when moving away is not possible. Once in that sector, students learn to use simple but effective techniques that serve to hook and trap the kicking leg. This leaves the attacker surprised and (by being on one leg) off-balance. The water principle is clearly employed here. The follow-up usually involves a fast and easy application of circular energy to take the attacker down. It is obvious that defenses against extremely low-level kicks simply do not exist. At best, the kick can be checked and somehow be absorbed by using your own legs. This may not be pleasant, but it will never take you out of the fight. The following techniques illustrate how combat hapkido handles midlevel or high kicks.

Defense Against a Front Kick

1. The attacker throws a front kick, so the defender steps into him in a diagonal direction and outside his guard. The defender uses his rear arm to catch the attacker's leg.

2. While keeping the attacker's leg trapped, the defender delivers a strike to the opponent's face.

3. With economy of movement, the defender just steps forward with his lead leg to off-balance the attacker.

4. This throws the attacker forward and to the ground.

Defense Against a Roundhouse Kick

1. The attacker throws a roundhouse kick. The defender steps inside of the attacker's guard and traps the attacker's leg with his rear arm.

2-3. He strikes the attacker's upper leg with his elbow to off-balance him.

Continued ▶

4. He then kicks low to the inside of the knee of the attacker's supporting leg. Note that this is a good decision tactically because the attacker can't defend against the kick.

5. This causes the attacker to fall to the ground.

CHAPTER 9
DEFENSE AGAINST WEAPONS

Attempting to disarm weapons is risky at best, always dangerous and sometimes foolish. Often, even when successfully applied, disarming techniques may still result in serious injuries for the defender. There are simply no guarantees. Disarming techniques require exceptional speed, accuracy, determination and courage, and they should be attempted only by self-defense practitioners who have acquired the necessary skills and confidence to execute them flawlessly. In any case, weapon-disarming techniques should be attempted only in extreme cases, as a last resort, when all other options are not available or would not be beneficial. Those options include negotiations, compliance, escape, cover and the use of improvised weapons. More than in any other group of techniques presented in this book, disarming techniques, because of their deadly implications, require the defender to truly possess a warrior mind-set with all its associated attributes.

Combat hapkido has classified disarming techniques into the following categories:

Edged weapons (static and dynamic)
Blunt weapons (always dynamic)
Handguns (always static)
Long firearms (always static)

Combat hapkido has also established a few basic rules to help students quickly understand the unique characteristics of dealing with weapons:

- You cannot disarm an attacker whom you cannot reach. If you are too far, use a different strategy or find a way to get close enough.
- When dealing with edged weapons, always grab and control the hand holding the weapon and not the weapon itself.
- When dealing with a firearm, always grab and control the weapon and not the hand holding it.
- When dealing with blunt weapons, you can grab and control the hand or the weapon or both.
- After the attacker has successfully been disarmed, move away so as not to allow him to try to regain the weapon.
- Unless absolutely necessary to protect your life, do not use the weapon you have just taken away from the attacker against him because he is now unarmed and the legal conditions have changed.

AGAINST A STATIC KNIFE

Defense Against a Static Knife to the Neck, No. 1

1. The attacker puts a knife to the left side of the defender's neck.

2. The defender moves his head away from the blade and widens his base. He grabs the attacker's weapon hand, using both hands to apply a very strong grip.

3. He then feigns a torque movement to the outside.

4. The defender suddenly reverses it to the inside, attempting to slash the attacker's neck with the blade.

5. He continues to torque inside.

6. The defender suddenly reverses again to the outside.

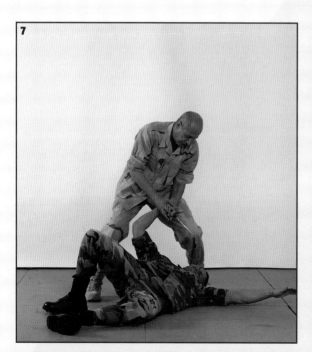

7. This helps him take the attacker down.

8. In the unlikely event that the attacker is still holding the knife, the defender removes it from his hand.

Defense Against a Static Knife to the Neck, No. 2

1. The attacker puts a knife to the right side of the defender's neck.

2. While moving his head away from the blade, the defender grabs the attacker's weapon hand with both his hands in a very strong grip. The defender also steps across and in front of the attacker while pulling the attacker's arm to his own body.

3. The defender drops his elbow on the attacker's elbow, placing him in an armbar.

4. From here, he is able to remove the knife.

Defense Against a Static Knife to the Throat From Behind (Hostage Situation)

1. The attacker grabs the defender from the back and places a knife at the defender's throat.

2. Lifting his chin away from the blade, the defender uses his two hands to grab the attacker's hand and forearm close to the wrist. At the same time, he drops into a wider and lower stance.

3. By stepping back and across and under the attacker's arm, the defender can escape.

4. He continues holding the attacker's arm tight across his chest to control the weapon.

Continued ➡

5. While he begins to apply a wrist lock, the defender kicks the attacker in the face or chest.

6. The defender can now remove the knife.

AGAINST A DYNAMIC KNIFE

Defense Against a Knife Thrust to the Center Mass

1. The attacker prepares to launch a thrusting strike to the defender's upper abdomen.

2. As he attacks, the defender moves his body back and into a wide stance. He then grabs the attacker's weapon hand with both his hands.

3. Keeping his elbows close to his body, the defender jerks the attacker's arm upward and applies a painful wrist lock.

4. The defender then steps across and under the attacker's arm.

Continued

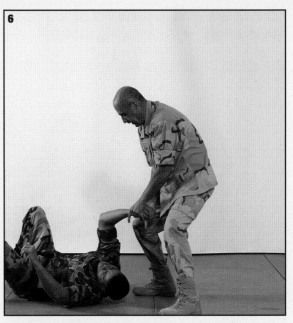

5. Placing the attacker's elbow on his shoulder, the defender cranks it down.

6. Passing the attacker's arm over his head, the defender executes a takedown.

Defense Against a Downward Stabbing Attack

1. The attacker prepares to launch an overhead knife strike.

2. As he does, the defender steps slightly sideways and forward while using both hands to deflect his strike.

3. Using his momentum, the defender pushes down the attacker's arm to grab the attacker's wrist.

4. Reverse angle: He secures the grip with both hands.

5. He steps across and behind the attacker's leg.

6. The defender applies a wrist lock and armbar to disarm his opponent.

Defense Against a Forehand Slash

1. The attacker prepares for a forehand upper-body slashing strike.

2. The defender steps in and intercepts the strike using both forearms—one to the side of the neck and the other to the attacker's weapon arm.

3. Then the defender traps the attacker's weapon arm with one arm and strikes the attacker's neck or face again with the other.

4. He steps across and behind the attacker's leg.

5. Using a low-line sweep, the defender takes the attacker down.

6. The defender then applies an armbar.

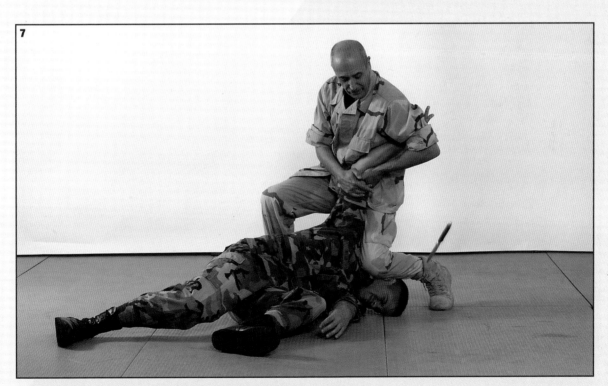

7. He continues to apply it until the attacker drops the weapon.

Defense Against a Backhand Slash

1. The attacker launches a wide forehand slashing strike that the defender is able to avoid by leaning back.

2. As the attacker prepares to follow up with a backhand slash, the defender steps in.

3. He moves behind the attacker while trapping the attacker's arm against his body.

4. The defender reaches around the attacker with the other arm to grab his wrist.

5. While pulling the attacker's arm across the attacker's neck, the defender begins to drop him to the ground backward.

6. When the attacker hits the ground, the defender applies a wrist lock.

7. The defender disarms the attacker.

AGAINST A BLUNT WEAPON

Defense Against an Overhead Strike

1. The attacker prepares to launch an overhead strike.

2. The defender steps slightly out and forward on the weapon side.

3. As the strike misses, the defender grabs the attacker's arm.

4. He twists it behind the attacker.

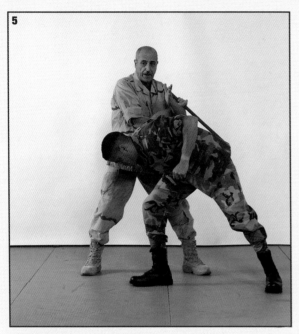

5. The defender then traps the attacker's arm inside his own.

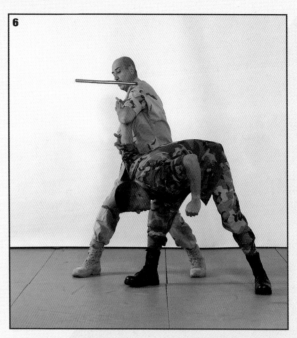

6. By cranking it forcefully and outward, the defender disarms the attacker.

Defense Against a Roundhouse Strike

1. The attacker prepares to launch a roundhouse strike.

2. The defender steps across and inside the attacker's guard and grabs his arm with both his hands.

Continued ➤

3. While lowering his body into a wider stance, the defender continues pulling the attacker forward.

4. He executes a hip throw.

5. When the attacker hits the ground, the defender removes the weapon.

AGAINST A HANDGUN

Defense Against a Handgun Pointed to the Head

1. The defender is confronted with a handgun to the face.

2. Dropping in a low and wide stance, he grabs the attacker's hand and the gun with both his hands and pushes upward, therefore clearing his head from the line of fire.

3. Maintaining a strong grip, the defender rotates the gun up and toward the attacker.

4-5. The resulting wrist lock will take the attacker down, allowing the defender to extract the weapon and move away.

 Continued

Cross-Hand Defense Against a Handgun Pointed to the Midsection

1. The defender is confronted with a handgun to the midsection.

2. While rotating his body away from the line of fire, the defender grabs the gun with his cross-hand.

3. He twists the gun clockwise and toward the attacker.

4. The wrist-and-finger lock will cause the attacker to go down while the defender extracts the weapon.

5. From there, the defender moves away.

Same-Side Defense Against a Handgun Pointed to the Midsection

1. In the same scenario as the previous technique, the defender is confronted with a handgun to the midsection.

2. This time, the defender grabs the gun with the same-side hand.

3. He twists the gun counterclockwise.

4. This causes a wrist lock.

5. The defender extracts the weapon and moves away.

Outside Defense Against a Handgun Pointed to the Back

1. The defender has a gun to his back.

2. He steps low and wide to the back. He wants to be close to the attacker.

Continued ▶

  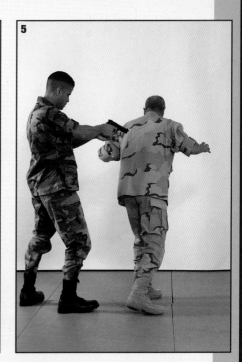

3-5. The defender must *NOT* step out or away, as shown above.

6. As he steps back outside of the attacker's guard, the defender strikes the face with his lead hand.

7. He pivots forward and traps the attacker's arm.

8. The defender strikes the attacker's face again.

9. The defender continues to apply pressure on the attacker's face by attacking his eyes with his fingers.

10-11. From there, the defender takes the attacker down while keeping the attacker's arm locked. The defender then disarms him.

Inside Defense Against a Handgun Pointed to the Back

1. The defender is confronted with the same scenario as the previous sequence.

2. He steps back and inside the attacker's guard to strike the attacker's face or throat with his lead forearm.

3. Pivoting forward, the defender traps his opponent's arm while striking the attacker's face again.

4. The defender steps across and behind the attacker's leg while keeping a grip on his throat.

5. He sweeps the attacker down while keeping his arm trapped.

6. Then the defender applies an armbar.

7. He extracts the weapon.

8. The defender moves away.

Defense Against a Handgun Pointed to the Head From Behind (Hostage Situation)

1. In this hostage-type situation, the defender is held at gunpoint to the head from behind.

2. He drops wider and moves his head forward.

3. While doing this, he simultaneously uses his cross-hand to strike the gun and hand of his attacker with all his power.

4. The idea is to smash the weapon into the attacker's face.

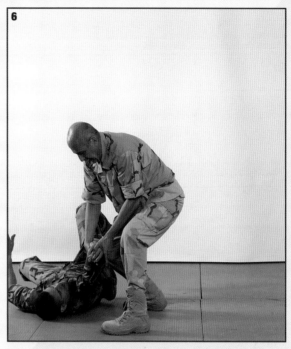

5. When the attacker recoils from the sudden strike, the defender, using both hands, grabs the attacker's gun and hand. The defender must maintain an extremely strong grab.

6. He then rotates out and takes the attacker down.

This close-up shows how the defender's hand smashes the gun into the attacker's face.

AGAINST LONG FIREARMS

Defense Against a Long Firearm Pointed to the Upper Torso

1. The defender is confronted with an assault rifle to his upper body.

2. Using his left hand to grab the barrel of the rifle, he pushes it high and into the attacker's face.

3. The defender immediately inserts his right hand into the position shown and grabs the butt of the rifle.

4. Continuing the counterclockwise motion, the defender smashes the barrel against the attacker's head.

5-6. He extracts the weapon and moves away.

Defense Against a Long Firearm Pointed to the Lower Torso

1. The rifle is pointed at the defender's stomach.

2. Using his left hand, the defender pushes the barrel away and grabs it.

3. Reaching across with his right hand, the defender grabs the top of the rifle's butt.

4. The defender extracts the weapon by rotating it clockwise.

5. The defender smashes it against the attacker's head.

Inside Defense Against a Long Firearm Pointed to the Back, No. 1

1. The rifle is pointed to the middle of the defender's back.

2. The defender steps back and inside of the attacker's guard. He hits the attacker in the face with his lead hand.

3. The defender wraps his right arm around the rifle.

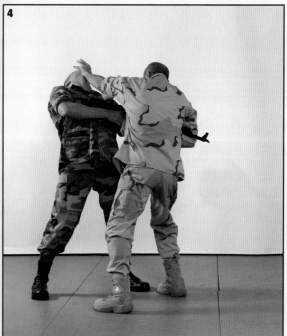

4. The defender hits the attacker's face again, this time with his left hand.

5

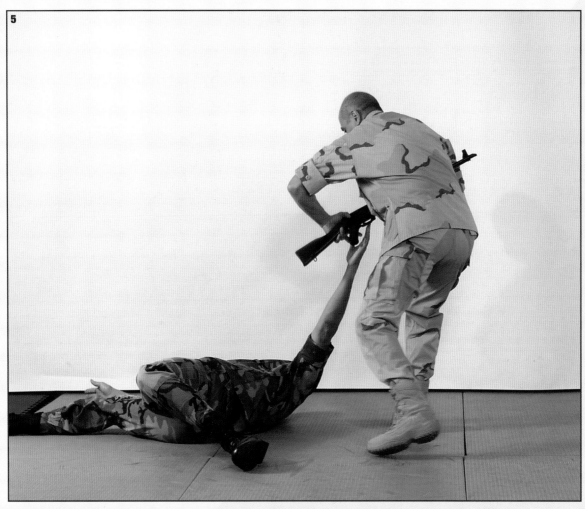

5. As the attacker goes down, he is forced to let go of the weapon trapped under the defender's arm.

Inside Defense Against a Long Firearm Pointed to the Back, No. 2

1. The rifle is pointed to the middle of the defender's back.

2. Like in the previous sequence, the defender strikes the attacker's face.

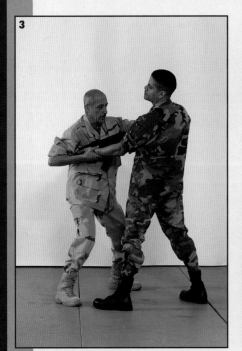

3. This time, after wrapping his arm around the rifle, the defender reaches with the other hand and grabs the top of the rifle's butt.

4. The defender extracts it by rotating out.

5. The defender then smashes the rifle's butt to the attacker's head.

Outside Defense Against a Long Firearm Pointed to the Back, No. 3

1. The rifle is pointed to the middle of the defender's back.

2. This time, the defender steps back and outside of the attacker's guard while striking the attacker's face with the left hand.

3. The defender wraps his left arm around the rifle.

4. Hitting the attacker's face again with his right hand, the defender then uses it to grab the butt of the rifle.

Continued ➤

5-6. The defender jerks the rifle clockwise to extract it.

   Weapons are, by definition, killing tools. I must stress again how dangerous it is to attempt to disarm an attacker who, by the very possession of a weapon, has already implicitly manifested his willingness to use it. Hard, serious training involving many repetitions with realistic (training) weapons is needed to achieve the level of technical proficiency and the speed—and let's not forget the warrior spirit—necessary to succeed.

EPILOGUE

This book presents only a portion of combat-*hapkido* concepts and techniques. They were selected from each category because they best illustrate the practical, no-nonsense approach of the system. Bear in mind that the official combat-hapkido curriculum, from white to black belt, contains 175 techniques. The advanced course up to sixth-degree black belt contains another 90. When you add to that the many variations, combinations and reversals as well as factor in the separate component courses—disarming, trapping, ground survival, pressure points, cane, *dan-bong*, etc.—you can easily see that the total system can keep you busy learning for a lifetime. That's the good news.

The other good news is that with a scientifically sound, practical, effective and reality-based self-defense system like combat hapkido, you do not have to be the student for a lifetime, although this is the preferred student of all martial arts instructors. Even if an individual can train for only a relatively short time, such as one or two years, he will acquire a significant set of basic skills and valuable defensive strategies.

If self-defense is your primary goal, reality-based training offers the best and shortest route. Therefore, with combat hapkido, you can have the best of both worlds: a self-defense art that you can use to defend yourself now and that will challenge you as you learn it over a lifetime.

"If you want peace, prepare for war."

—Anonymous

ABOUT THE AUTHOR

Grandmaster John Pellegrini has more than 40 years of martial arts training, beginning his study of judo and karate in his native Italy in 1966. He served in the elite 1st Airborne Regiment of the Italian Army—NATO Forces from 1968 to 1969.

Moving to the United States in 1970, he pursued a career in law enforcement, corporate security, investigations and executive protection until 1987, when he became a full-time martial arts instructor operating a chain of schools in Florida. In 1992, he founded the International Combat Hapkido Federation to promote and regulate his martial arts style of combat *hapkido*, which is now being taught in more than 250 charter branches in 12 countries.

Pellegrini holds a ninth-degree black belt in hapkido and a ninth-degree black belt in *taekwondo*. He is also a certified instructor in *aikido* and *jeet kune do*. He has been inducted in more than 20 martial arts halls of fame and received numerous honors, including 2004 *Black Belt* Instructor of the Year, 2004 *Tae Kwon Do Times* Hapkido Instructor of the Year, 2005 *Budo International* magazine Legend Grandmaster and 2001 *Action Martial Arts Magazine* Outstanding Contribution to the Martial Arts.

Pellegrini has been featured in many newspapers and magazines, including *The Wall Street Journal*. In the martial arts media, he has been on the cover of 17 magazines around the world, including *Black Belt* in June 2003 and January 2009. Today, he is one of the most sought-after seminar leaders, traveling the world more than 40 weekends a year. His combat-hapkido system is extremely popular with law enforcement and the military. He has trained U.S. troops in Afghanistan in 2006 and in Iraq in 2008. Pellegrini resides in the Phoenix area with his family.

TESTIMONIALS

"I am extremely proud of grandmaster Pellegrini's latest accomplishment in publishing this book on combat *hapkido*. He has been my student and friend since 1992, and during this time, I have witnessed his hard work, dedication and professionalism in his quest to grow hapkido around the world. It has been a great reward for me to know that my support and guidance have contributed to his success in the martial arts."

—Grandmaster In Sun Seo, 10th *Dan*, Chairman,
World Kido Federation/Hanminjok Hapkido Association

"I have known my friend John Pellegrini for over 20 years, and we have worked together many times teaching joint seminars in the United States, Ireland and Finland. I can state with absolute confidence that his combat-hapkido system really works!"

—Bill Wallace, Former Kickboxing World Champion

"I have been in the martial arts for over 40 years. When I met grandmaster Pellegrini in 1998, I was a sixth dan in traditional hapkido, but I was so impressed by combat hapkido that I immediately adopted it and made my cane system part of his organization. When it comes to realistic self-defense, nothing comes close to the style grandmaster Pellegrini has developed."

—Grandmaster Mark Shuey Sr., Founder, Cane Masters

"Serving as a law-enforcement officer for more than 20 years and as a regional training academy director, I have found that the techniques of the combat-hapkido system provide the most versatile and complete levels of control and self-protection. They are adaptable to any situation and consistent with the use-of-force continuum."

—Daniel K. Allen, Chief of Police, Argentine Township Police Department, Michigan

"By going against the traditional martial arts establishment, grandmaster Pellegrini has stirred up his share of controversy. I applaud him for being a courageous maverick. In fact, we got to know each other because I was going through a tough time dealing with nasty politics in a repressive system. As fellow rebels, we became good friends and over the years have done several seminars together. Grandmaster Pellegrini is an excellent, top-notch technician and an open-minded, wise teacher."

—W. Hock Hochheim, Combatives Expert

"I have personally studied under grandmaster Pellegrini for several years and believe that combat hapkido is the most realistic and effective martial arts system available. I have been deployed to numerous locations throughout the world and find that combat-hapkido techniques have contributed to my combat readiness and physical well-being."

—James W. Redmore, Command Sergeant Major, U.S. Army

"Everyone should study under grandmaster John Pellegrini. Combat hapkido is a must for every martial artist. In my book, grandmaster John Pellegrini is one of the most knowledgeable and respected martial arts teachers today. I loved the book and so will you."

—Cynthia Rothrock, Martial Artist, Actress and 1983 *Black Belt*
Hall of Fame Female Competitor of the Year

Logo courtesy of John Pellegrini